RESEARCH

REPORTS

A GUIDE FOR MIDDLE AND HIGH SCHOOL STUDENTS

BY
HELEN SULLIVAN
AND LINDA SERNOFF

THE MILLBROOK PRESS   BROOKFIELD, CONNECTICUT

Authors' Note   We would like to thank those who helped us as we wrote this book. Foremost is Lise Markl, who contributed the information about the various on-line data sources as well as the information about the ways in which a computer can be used to produce a report. Her technological expertise and editing suggestions are greatly appreciated.

We are grateful to Herb Levine for acting as our mentor from the very beginning stages of the book. Herb, in addition to Kathie Loving, Thomas Mann, and Jane Reynolds Toelkes, provided us with invaluable suggestions and pertinent materials for which we are indebted.

Last, but not least, we wish to thank Elizabeth Allison Sernoff and Brian Lehman for their encouragement and moral support.

Published by The Millbrook Press
2 Old New Milford Road, Brookfield, Connecticut 06804

Library of Congress Cataloging-in-Publication Data
Sullivan, Helen.
Research and report writing: a guide for middle and high school students / by Helen Sullivan and Linda Sernoff
p.   cm.
Includes bibliographical references (p.   ) and index.
Summary: Clear, concise directions, logical and sequential organization, and numerous examples painlessly guide the student through every step of the report process.
ISBN 1-56294-694-3 (lib. bdg.)   ISBN 0-7613-0398-7 (pbk.)
1. Report writing. 2. Research—United States. 3. Education, Secondary—United States.
I. Sernoff, Linda. II. Title.
LB1047.3.S85   1996
373.13'028'1—dc20   95-21489   CIP

CONTENTS

FOREWORD

I could have used this book myself when I was in high school. Most of the papers I wrote then were much more oriented toward analysis of a topic rather than research about it, and that wasn't due to brilliant analytical skills so much as to my profound ignorance of how to do research.

Two of the techniques presented in this well-focused book are especially useful, but I didn't catch on to them myself until graduate school. The first is thinking of library sources in terms of types of literature (encyclopedias, yearbooks, handbooks, indexes, biographical sources, and so on). If you know in advance that certain distinct kinds of reference sources exist, that each is particularly good for answering certain types of questions, and that a wide array of such types of literature can be found within any subject area, then you will have surprising power to move around comfortably within the literature of a variety of subjects—even those that you know nothing about beforehand.

The second technique is interviewing people. The worst advice I ever received as a student—and I heard it several times—

was, "You shouldn't have to bother people with questions; if you can't find the information on your own, you're no scholar." I am delighted that Ms. Sullivan and Ms. Sernoff have the eminent good sense to realize that the best researchers ask the most questions, not the fewest, and that this book provides practical advice on how to exploit the people sources who are so often much more informative than any library. Most important, though, is the basic point: It's OK to ask. If someone is uncooperative, then just go on to somebody else. From Sherlock Holmes and Nancy Drew to V.I. Warshawski and the heroines of R.L. Stine, nobody ever solved a mystery without asking a few questions. If you absorb that message alone, and act on it, *Research Reports* will have more than repaid the time you spend with it.

Thomas Mann
Reference Librarian
Author of *A Guide to Library Research Methods*
and *Library Research Models*

PREFACE

The purpose of *Research Reports: A Guide for Middle and High School Students* is to make it easy for you to write a research report. This book will guide you step by step through the research process from choosing a topic to producing the final report.

Easy readability, clear concise directions, and numerous examples painlessly guide you through every step of the report process. Logical and sequential organization with sample outlines, captivating introductory and concluding paragraphs, as well as a sample report, immediately provide the ease and confidence necessary to write a report successfully.

The authors clearly recognize the merits of computers. Guidelines for using the various functions of computers, from taking notes to conducting database searches, are an invaluable feature of this book.

Research Reports: A Guide for Middle and High School Students can be used as a guide, a reference book, or a textbook. Students, teachers, parents, and librarians will find it indispensable.

CHAPTER 1
INTRODUCTION
TO REPORT
WRITING

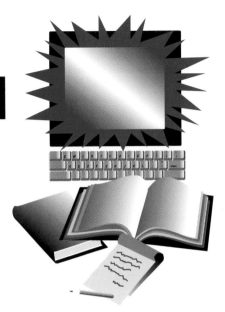

A research report is an in-depth account about a specific topic. It is based upon facts and information collected as a result of a thorough study of the topic.

Teachers assign research reports for a number of reasons. One reason is to have you search for information so that you will learn a great deal about a specific topic. A second and more practical reason teachers assign research reports is to enable you to become better acquainted with the reference sources available in libraries and elsewhere.

Learning how to research and write a good report now will provide you with skills and experience that will be beneficial to you when you go on to college.

NECESSARY STEPS

This book will help you write your research report. It will guide you, step by step, through the research process. The book is organized in the sequence of the basic steps you follow when you are assigned a report:

1. Choose a topic if one is not assigned to you.

2. Inquire and read about the topic to help you decide what is important and of interest.

3. Develop an outline.

4. Locate information.

5. Take notes.

6. Repeat steps 4 and 5 until you are satisfied that you have enough information.

7. Write a draft.

8. Edit and revise to improve your draft.

9. Repeat steps 7 and 8 until you are satisfied that you have written a clear, concise, and interesting report.

10. Prepare a title page and a bibliography.

11. Prepare a good, clean final copy of the report.

12. Reread your final copy to be sure it is free of errors.

Details about how to proceed with each of these steps can be found in the following chapters of this guide. Remember that your teacher may have specific preferences or rules about sources you can use and formats for your footnotes, bibliography, and final copy. You may be required to turn in your outline, notes, or draft for approval before proceeding to the next step.

The widespread use of computers has broadened the sources of information available to many students. Computers can also simplify some steps in preparing a report, especially developing an outline and editing and revising your draft; however, the steps in the following chapters will help you whether you are using a computer or not. You do not need a computer to do good research or to write a good report.

CHAPTER 2
SELECTING A TOPIC

It is important to select a topic that interests you. Writing a report takes time and requires work; you will do your best work if you are interested in your topic.

If your teacher gives you the opportunity to choose your topic and you need ideas, go to the library and consult reference books that contain lists of possible topics. Two such books are *What Can I Write About?* by David Powell (National Council of Teachers of English, 1981), which contains 7,000 topics appropriate for students in grades 7–12, and *10,000 Ideas for Term Papers, Projects, Reports, and Speeches* by Kathryn Lamm (Prentice Hall, 3rd ed., 1991). Another source is *The Reference Shelf*, a series of paperbacks on topics of current interest, published by H.W. Wilson. Each contains excerpts from periodicals, books, and government documents and includes a bibliography that can help you start your research.

PRELIMINARY SEARCH FOR INFORMATION

Once you have a topic in mind, you will need to conduct a preliminary search for information. This will involve a trip to a library to look in encyclopedias, the card catalog, and specific books as well as on-line databases, if you have access to them, to see how much information is available. This search will help you decide whether or not you will be able to find enough information to write a good research report.

The key to finding information in any source is knowing what words to look under. In card catalogs and on-line catalogs, you usually look under subject headings like those used by the Library of Congress. For printed materials like books, you usually look in an index or a table of contents to find the headings used to organize the information. For electronic materials like CD-ROM packages and on-line databases, you may be able to use an electronic index, if the material has one, or you may need to try subject headings you have already found in printed materials.

STEP-BY-STEP PLAN

Begin your search by looking in a reference book that contains subject headings. A book of subject headings lists the words you need to search under to find information about a topic. Most libraries have the *Library of Congress Subject Headings* and organize the card catalog or on-line catalog by these headings. For example, if you were looking for information about Elvis Presley, you will find that PRESLEY, ELVIS is a Library of Congress subject heading.

Next, look in the index volumes of different sets of encyclopedias. The index volume, usually the last volume in the encyclopedia set, contains a list of the topics in the set as well as the volume and page numbers where information related to each topic can be found. For example, if you were thinking of writing about Elvis Presley you would use the following steps.

STEP 1

Look for the word PRESLEY in the index volume. For example, *World Book Encyclopedia* lists the following information under **Presley**:

> **Presley, Elvis** [American singer] **P:776** *with portrait*
> Rock music (The emergence of rock 'n' roll) **R:377** *with picture*
> Tennessee (Places to visit) **T:144** *with picture*
> United States *picture on* **U:110**
> **Presley Birthplace** [Tupelo]
> Mississippi (Places to visit) **M:632** *with picture*

STEP 2

Write down the volume and page numbers where information related to Elvis Presley can be found.

Examples:

Vol.	*Pg.*
P	776
R	377
T	144
U	110
M	632

STEP 3

Look in each of the volumes you listed. For example, you would look to see if the article about Elvis Presley's birthplace is brief or extensive and if the information might be useful to you.

STEP 4

Put a check mark beside the volumes and pages that would be useful. Draw a line through those that would not.

After checking the index volumes of encyclopedias, you should look at the library's catalog systems—card, computer on-line, microfilm, or microfiche—to determine the number of available books related to your topic. Many public libraries and some school libraries have on-line catalogs as well as card catalogs. The on-line catalog in such libraries usually contains more recent materials (typically those the library has acquired since about 1980), while the card catalog is kept for older materials (materials usually acquired before 1980).

Both kinds of catalogs are organized alphabetically by subject, title, and author; a card catalog may file subject cards separately from title and author cards. In a card catalog you find a source by looking in the appropriate alphabetized drawer; in an on–line catalog you find a source by choosing the type of search (subject, title, author, and sometimes key words) and entering the appropriate information. In an on-line catalog you may also be able to narrow or broaden the search to locate more specific or more general materials. You do this by "limiting" a subject with certain key words or by combining key words for different subjects.

For example, if you were thinking of writing about nuclear weapons you might look under WEAPONS, NUCLEAR ARMA-MENT, and/or WARFARE. If you find too much material, you can narrow your search by looking under a more specific aspect; for example, NUCLEAR ARMAMENT—INTERNATIONAL AGREE-

MENTS. In an on-line catalog, you may be able to limit your search by other characteristics such as the year the information was published.

After you find the titles, follow these steps:

STEP 5

Write down the call numbers of the books listed. Most of them will begin with the same three digits. Some on-line catalogs allow you to print out a list of titles.

STEP 6

Locate these books and briefly look at the table of contents and the index of each book to see if the book would be helpful to you.

You may also look at encyclopedias or databases on CD-ROM if they are available. Encyclopedias on CD-ROM are organized much like encyclopedias in print; to find subject headings, look in the index. CD-ROM databases may consist of an index of periodical references or the full text of the articles. They usually have an index called a thesaurus, a list of the terms under which the information on the disk is indexed; it may be a separate file on the disk, or it may be a printed list. You can search them as you would an on-line catalog. When the search is complete, you will have a list of references or a list of articles that are on the disk. You may be able to print out this list.

Another source to check for preliminary information on topics that involve current events is a database in an on-line service such as America Online, CompuServe, Prodigy, GEnie, or Dow Jones News/Retrieval. These services organize their databases in different ways; they may be called "libraries," or they may be accessible through discussion groups in specific interest areas. You can search for information about your topic in a database in the same way that you would in a CD-ROM package, by subject headings and key words.

You may also be able to get information from the Internet, but because of its size and complexity you will probably not find the Internet useful for this preliminary search. If your library has access to the Internet, ask your librarian for help. He or she can help you determine whether and how to conduct your search.

After you have looked in a number of encyclopedias, books, and databases, you will know if you can find enough information for your report. If there is not enough information you will have to select a different topic and conduct another preliminary search for information. If there is a huge amount of information about your topic, you will need to narrow the focus of your topic.

NARROWING THE FOCUS

You may find that the topic you want to write about is so broad that you do not know where to begin or end. If this happens, choose a smaller portion of that topic. For example, if you are studying the continent of Antarctica and decide to write a report about it, you would soon realize that Antarctica is too broad a topic for a single report. In this case you should select one aspect of Antarctica for your report; that topic might be exploration of the continent within the past fifty years, or animal life on the continent. You could narrow the topic of animal life even further by focusing on one specific animal in Antarctica, such as the penguin.

Once you have decided on the topic of your report, you are ready to write your title or thesis statement. The following definitions and examples will help you decide which is appropriate for your report.

TITLE

A title lets the reader know the topic of your report; for example:

The Assassination of John Fitzgerald Kennedy

Chemical and Biological Warfare

Elvis Presley

THESIS STATEMENT

A thesis statement lets the reader know the topic about which you are going to draw a conclusion based upon the evidence you found in your research.

Usually, high school and college teachers expect you to prove a point in your report. Therefore, you make a thesis statement consisting of a point of view about your chosen topic, which you support or "prove" with evidence found in your research. Some sample thesis statements are:

Who Is Responsible for the Death of John Fitzgerald Kennedy?

Can the Use of Chemical and Biological Weapons Ever Be Justified?

Elvis Presley Lives On in the Music of Others

CHAPTER 3 FORMING AN OUTLINE

The key to a good report is a strong outline. The outline becomes a tool that helps you organize your thoughts and decide what information you are going to present. For this reason, many teachers require that their students submit an outline for suggestions and approval before taking notes or writing their reports. You may want to expand upon your original outline as you research your topic in depth, with the final outline becoming the table of contents.

OUTLINING WITH A COMPUTER OR WORD PROCESSOR

Developing and revising an outline on paper can require a lot of rewriting. Most common word processing software packages simplify this task with an outline function that lets you create, change, and reorganize your outline easily, renumbering it automatically.

If you are using a word processor, you need to consider how to set up your files to make it easy for you to work on your report and keep your notes organized. With a very basic program, you may need to create a separate file for each major topic in your outline. If the program can create "summaries" for each file, you should enter information in the "subject," "key word," or "abstract" fields that will identify which parts of your report the file contains.

The outline function in some word-processing programs will let you expand and collapse the outline so you can easily move from subtopic to subtopic. In these programs you build directly on the outline by typing your draft under the subtopic heading; then, if you want to reorganize the outline, you can easily cut and paste the sections. Look in the software menus for "Outlining" and use the "Help" command or your manual to find out how to use the outline function.

If your report is very long (more than thirty pages), or if you are writing a report with a partner or a group, you may want to use a word-processing function that lets you create "master documents" based on your outline. This function makes it easier to work on longer and more complicated reports by breaking them into smaller pieces linked in one large file. Not all word-processing software can perform this function. Use the "Help" command or your manual to find out whether the function is available and how to use it.

STEP-BY-STEP PLAN

The following steps will help you develop your outline.

STEP 1

Write down or type into a computer all the things you and others may want to know about your topic. Begin by asking yourself WHO, WHAT, WHEN, WHERE, WHY, and HOW? For example, if you were writing about capital punishment, you would probably make a list of questions such as the following:

What is capital punishment?

Is it morally right to take the life of another human being?

Is capital punishment a deterrent?

How has the Supreme Court ruled in regard to the death penalty?

Which constitutional amendments address capital punishment?

What methods are used to carry out the death penalty?

Have people ever been given the death penalty based upon circumstantial evidence?

Does capital punishment unfairly target minorities?

How can we be sure that innocent people are not executed?

Do the laws vary from state to state in regard to the death penalty?

Should a mentally deficient person be sentenced to death?

Should an insane person be sentenced to death?

Is murder in a "kill or be killed" situation taken into account before the death penalty is imposed?

How many states have a death penalty?

How many states have abolished the death penalty?

How long should a person be subjected to a wait on death row?

Does capital punishment unfairly target the poor?

Should juveniles be executed?

Does capital punishment violate the Constitution?

How much does it cost to execute a criminal?

What is the average wait on death row?

How many of those sentenced to death try to kill themselves?

What are the ways in which the death penalty is carried out?

How can a destitute criminal hire a lawyer to file an appeal?

What is the average annual cost to imprison a criminal?

Is it fair to execute the head of a family and leave the family as secondary victims?

Is there a difference in crime rates between states with the death penalty and those without it?

What do I want to "prove" about capital punishment?

STEP 2

Reread your questions and decide upon as few words as possible to summarize each question.

DEFINITION — What is capital punishment?

MORALITY — Is it morally right to take the life of another human being?

DETERRENT — Is capital punishment a deterrent?

SUPREME COURT DECISIONS — How has the Supreme Court ruled in regard to the death penalty?

U.S. CONSTITUTION — Which constitutional amendments address capital punishment?

CRUEL AND UNUSUAL — What methods are used to carry out the death penalty?

CIRCUMSTANTIAL EVIDENCE — Have people ever been given the death penalty based upon circumstantial evidence?

MINORITIES — Does capital punishment unfairly target minorities?

IRREVERSIBILITY — How can we be sure that innocent people are not executed?

STATE LAWS — Do the laws vary from state to state in regard to the death penalty?

MENTAL DEFICIENCY — Should a mentally deficient person be sentenced to death?

INSANITY — Should an insane person be sentenced to death?

SELF-PRESERVATION — Is murder in a "kill or be killed" situation taken into account before the death penalty is imposed?

RETENTIONIST STATES	How many states have a death penalty?
ABOLITIONIST STATES	How many states have abolished the death penalty?
DEATH ROW WAIT	How long should a person be subjected to a wait on death row?
INEQUALITY	Does capital punishment unfairly target the poor?
CHRONOLOGICAL AGE	Should juveniles be executed?
U.S. CONSTITUTION	Does capital punishment violate the Constitution?
ECONOMIC	How much does it cost to execute a criminal?
DEATH ROW WAIT	What is the average wait on death row?
DEATH ROW WAIT	How many of those sentenced to death try to kill themselves?
METHODS	What are the ways in which the death penalty is carried out?
IMPOVERISHMENT	How can a destitute criminal hire a lawyer to file an appeal?
ECONOMIC	What is the average annual cost to imprison a criminal?
VICTIMS' FAMILIES	Is it fair to execute the head of a family and leave the family as secondary victims?
CRIME RATE	Is there a difference in crime rates between states with the death penalty and those without it?
THESIS	What do I want to "prove" about capital punishment?

STEP 3

Group the words that are related.

Definition
Thesis

Supreme Court Decisions
U.S. Constitution
State Laws
Abolitionist States
Retentionist States

Cruel and Unusual
Inequality
Morality
Minorities
Irreversibility
Mental Deficiency
Insanity
Self-Preservation
Circumstantial Evidence
Death Row Wait
Chronological Age
Methods
Impoverishment
Victims' Families

Deterrent
Economic
Crime Rate

STEP 4

Organize these groups of words to form a basic outline adding topics and subtopics if necessary.

I. Introduction
   A. Definition
   B. Thesis
II. Legal Issues
   A. U.S. Constitution
   B. Position of Supreme Court
   C. Position of States
      1. Abolitionist States
      2. Retentionist States
III. Moral Issues
   A. Cruel and Unusual
      1. Methods of Execution
      2. Death Row Wait
   B. Inequality
      1. Minorities
      2. Impoverishment
      3. State Laws
   C. Irreversibility
      1. Innocent Victims
      2. Victims' Families
   D. Mitigating Circumstances
      1. Self-Preservation
      2. Circumstantial Evidence
      3. Mental Deficiency
      4. Insanity
      5. Chronological Age
IV. Effectiveness
   A. Deterrent
      1. Crime Rate in Abolitionist States
      2. Crime Rate in Retentionist States
   B. Economic Factors
V. Summary and Conclusion

You will change and expand the outline as you read and take notes. For example, your final outline for the example might look like the following:

CAPITAL PUNISHMENT

I. Introduction
    A. Capital Punishment Defined
    B. Thesis Statement
II. Legal Issues
    A. U.S. Constitution
        1. 8th Amendment
        2. 14th Amendment
    B. Position of Supreme Court
        1. 1972 Decision
        2. 1976 Decision
    C. Position of States
        1. Number of Abolitionist States
        2. Number of Retentionist States
III. Moral Issues
    A. Cruel and Unusual Punishment
        1. Methods of Execution
            a) Electrocution
            b) Lethal Injection
            c) Gas Chamber
            d) Firing Squad
            e) Hanging
        2. Death Row Wait
            a) Suicide Attempts
            b) Length of Stay Awaiting Execution
    B. Inequality
        1. Minorities
        2. Impoverishment
        3. Diversity of State Laws
    C. Irreversibility
        1. Execution of Innocent Victims
        2. Suffering of Victims' Families
    D. Mitigating Circumstances
        1. Self-Preservation
        2. Circumstantial Evidence

3. Mental Deficiency
4. Insanity
5. Chronological Age
IV. Effectiveness
  A. Deterrent
    1. Capital Crime Rate in Abolitionist States
    2. Capital Crime Rate in Retentionist States
  B. Economic Factors
    1. Cost of Life Imprisonment
    2. Cost of Execution
V. Summary and Conclusion

STEP-BY-STEP PLAN FOR A BIOGRAPHICAL REPORT

If you are writing about a person, follow the same steps:

STEP 1

Your list of questions may be like the following:

Why is the person famous?

What did the person invent, make, write, discover, or do to become famous?

When was the person born?

Where was the person born?

What steps led to the work/discovery?

Who influenced the person's life?

Where did the person go to school?

How has the work/discovery affected our lives?

What other works/discoveries were made as a result of the person's original invention/discovery?

Did the person have an unusual childhood?

Did the person marry and have children?

When did the person die?

At what age did the person die?

How did the person become interested in his or her work?

What did the person do in retirement?

Who were the person's parents?

Were there any brothers or sisters?

How did the person learn about his or her field?

What was his or her first work/discovery?

When did the person begin to teach?

Where did the person teach?

Who studied under the person?

When did the person retire?

STEP 2

Reread your questions and decide upon one or two words that summarize each question.

DISCOVERY	Why is the person famous?
DISCOVERY	What did the person discover to become famous?
PLACE OF BIRTH	Where was the person born?
DATE OF BIRTH	When was the person born?
PRE-WORK/DISCOVERY EVENTS	What steps led to the work/discovery?

INFLUENTIAL PEOPLE	Who influenced the person's life?
SCHOOLING	Where did the person go to school?
EFFECTS OF WORK/ DISCOVERY	How has the person's discovery affected our lives?
LATER WORK/ DISCOVERIES	What other discoveries were made as a result?
CHILDHOOD	Did the person have an unusual childhood?
MARITAL STATUS	Did the person marry and have children?
DATE OF DEATH	When did the person die?
LIFE SPAN	At what age did the person die?
INFLUENTIAL EVENTS	How did the person become interested in his or her work?
RETIREMENT	What did the person do in retirement?
PARENTS	Who were the person's parents?
SIBLINGS	Were there any brothers or sisters?
EDUCATION	How did the person learn about his or her field?
FIRST WORK/DISCOVERY	What was his or her first work/discovery?
CAREER CHANGE	When did the person begin to teach?
PROFESSORSHIP	Where did the person teach?
FAMOUS STUDENTS	Who studied under the person?
RETIREMENT	When did the person retire?

STEP 3

Group the words that are related.

Childhood
Date of Birth
Place of Birth
Parents
Siblings

Education
Schooling
Influential People
Influential Events

Discovery
Effects of Discovery
Pre–Discovery Events
First Discovery
Later Discoveries

Date of Death
Life Span
Marital Status
Retirement
Professorship
Famous Students
Career Change

STEP 4

Organize these groups of words to form a basic outline, adding topics and subtopics if necessary.

    I. Early Years
       A. Date of Birth
       B. Place of Birth
       C. Parents
       D. Siblings
   II. School Years
       A. Education
       B. Influential People
          1. Teachers
          2. Mentors
       C. Influential Events
  III. Working Years
       A. Pre-Discovery Events
       B. First Discovery
          1. Immediate Effects
          2. Present-Day Effects
       C. Subsequent Discoveries
  IV. Later Years
       A. Marital Status
       B. Career Change
          1. Professorship
          2. Famous Students
       C. Retirement
       D. Life Span
       E. Date of Death

CHAPTER 4
RESEARCHING
FOR
INFORMATION

When you look for and collect facts and information about a topic, you are doing research. The purpose of research is to learn as much as possible about a specific topic in the time available. This is accomplished by using authoritative books, encyclopedias, computer databases, and other reference materials containing factual information to ensure that your report contains accurate and up-to-date information. It is also accomplished by interviewing people who are knowledgeable about the topic to obtain details not available in reference materials and to gain perspective on the topic (see Chapter 5).

REFERENCE OPTIONS

In most instances the reference materials you need can be found in your school and public libraries. Be sure to ask librarians for their assistance; they are very familiar with reference materials in their libraries and are experts in locating information. Depending on the topic of your report, it may be beneficial to contact an embassy, an office of tourism, or a professional organization for information. A librarian can assist you in finding the appropriate addresses or telephone numbers. In addition, through a process called interlibrary loan, a librarian can arrange to borrow from another library books and other reference materials not available at your local library.

Printed materials—books, encyclopedias, and periodicals such as magazines and newspapers—are the main sources of information for most school reports. Magazines and newspapers may also be archived on microfilm or microfiche. Printed materials are free and easy to use. Electronic materials—on-line databases and CD-ROM packages—may also be used in your school or public library or at home, if computers are available. These databases can be accessed through on-line information services and through the Internet.

Although it contains vast amounts of information, the Internet will probably not be useful. Its complexity requires an understanding of sophisticated computer search tools. In addition, you can only access it through certain providers, such as universities, government agencies, and similar organizations. Some libraries may have access to the Internet; in those that do, a librarian or experienced researcher will usually do the actual search.

On-line database services usually charge a fee for use, while a library may or may not charge for use of CD-ROM packages. Using electronic materials almost always requires some training, although some basic concepts apply to all. If your library has electronic materials, a librarian can help you. Refer to Appendix A for a complete listing and description of reference sources that you may find in your library. The listing gives detailed information about general and subject encyclopedias, almanacs and yearbooks, statistical sources, handbooks and manuals, magazine and newspaper indexes, biographical indexes and directories, and government publications.

Printed and electronic materials are not the only sources of information. Interviews are excellent sources of firsthand information, particularly in regard to important historical events. When you mention your topic to people, you will often find that they will refer you to people and sources you would not have discovered on your own. The same will be true of the reading you do; one publication will refer to other publications with additional and sometimes more significant information.

THE PRELIMINARY SEARCH

Your preliminary search for information will familiarize you with the types of headings used for your topic. If you do not find enough materials on your topic under a specific subject heading, try related terms. For example, if you are writing about Thomas Edison's invention of a movie camera, you might look under MOVIES, or you might need to look under MOVING PICTURES, MOTION PICTURES, FILM, or CINEMA. You might also look under EDISON, THOMAS. If you find a great amount of material on your topic, narrow the focus to a particular aspect of that topic. In this example, you might look under MOVIES—INVENTION.

For electronic materials like CD-ROM packages and on-line databases, you can refine your search for information even further. Most electronic resources can be searched by key words in addition to the subject, title, or author. Many CD-ROMs, for example, allow you to search for words within an article in addition to those in the title. This type of search can find a resource you might have otherwise missed; it can also find too many resources.

As with printed materials, when you find an abundance of information on electronic materials, you must focus your search. You do this by adding key words to the subject, combining them so the search finds only those sources that include all the key words. If you don't find enough material, you can broaden your search by using other key words so the search finds all sources that include any one of the words you specify. When in doubt, ask a librarian to help you determine if you are using the appropriate words.

STEP-BY-STEP PLAN

When you are ready to begin your research, follow these steps:

STEP 1

Take the following with you to your school or public library:

> 5- by 8-inch index cards (or 8½- by 11-inch sheets of paper)
>
> 3- by 5-inch index cards

The large cards (or papers) are for taking notes; the small ones are for compiling information for your bibliography.

STEP 2

Go to the library and talk to the librarian in charge of the reference section. Explain the topic of your research so that he or she can help you determine and locate the best reference sources.

STEP 3

Start with a set of encyclopedias. Look for the topic of your report in the Index Volume to see which volumes in the set have information about your topic. Often, information about a topic will appear in more than one of the volumes. When using an encyclopedia on CD-ROM or on-line, look in the index or the-saurus for the topic of your report.

E X A M P L E : (from *World Book Encyclopedia*)

Kennedy, John Fitzgerald [U.S. President]
    K:260 *with pictures*
    See also the Reading and Study Guide on this topic
    Arlington National Cemetery **A:716**
    Berlin (An isolated city) **B:265**
    Cabinet (Membership) **C:3–4**
    Cold War (The Cuban missile crisis) **Ci:767**
    Cuba (The Bay of Pigs invasion) **Ci:1179**: (The Cuban
      missile crisis) **Ci:1179**
    Democratic Party (The New Frontier) **D:130**
    Guantánamo **G:435**
    Johnson, Lyndon Baines **J:144**: (Vice President) **J:148**
    Kennedy, Robert Francis **K:270**
    Nixon, Richard Milhous (Defeat by Kennedy)
      N:435–436 *with picture*
    Oswald, Lee Harvey **O:875**
    Patriotism **P:198**
    Peace Corps (History) **P:208**
    Pearson, Lester Bowles *picture on* **P:223**
    Television (The 1960's) **T:127**
    Texas (The mid-1900's) **T:208**
    United Nations (The Cuban missile crisis) **U:85**
    United States, History of the (The civil rights movement)
      U:182
    Vietnam War (The Viet Cong rebellion) **V:391**
    Warren Report **W:37**
    White House (Rebuilding and redecorating) **W:292**

When using an on-line database, you will have a variety of options to search for information related to your topic. Some databases let you use a mouse to click on icons to locate information; others require you to enter a command. Make sure you understand how to use the database before you start your search. Most consumer on-line services provide directions in the first menus of their databases or "libraries." If your library has access to academic databases, a librarian can help you with your search.

STEP 4

Write down the volume(s) and page number(s) before returning the Index Volume to the shelf.

EXAMPLES:

Kennedy, John

Vol.	Pg.
A	716
B	265
C	3–4
Ci	767, 1179
D	130
G	435
J	144, 148
K	260, 270
N	435–436
O	875
P	198, 208, 223
T	127, 208
U	85, 182
V	391
W	37, 292

If you are using a CD-ROM or on-line service, the computer will produce a list of citations or articles that match your key words. Some list only those titles that include your key words, while others list every article that has your key words in the text. You may be able to print this list. You may be able to save it in a separate file, which will save time if you are compiling your bibliography on a word processor. Some databases allow you to print the full text of the material you have found, or save it in a separate file to look at later on another computer. Take care—this can be expensive and can produce more information than you need.

STEP 5

Find each of the volumes on your list and turn to the page numbers you wrote down. If you are using a CD-ROM or on-line database, use the commands on the screen to open the first article you want to read. Now you are ready to begin to take notes for your report.

CHAPTER 5
TAKING NOTES
AND GATHERING
INFORMATION
FOR THE
BIBLIOGRAPHY

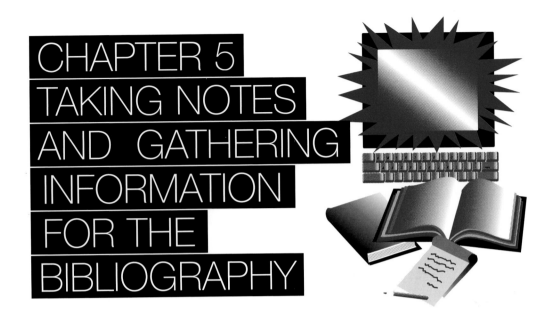

You take notes to help you remember the important information you want to include in your report and to ensure that what you write is accurate.

USING YOUR OUTLINE TO ORGANIZE NOTES

When you take notes, write or type only the facts you want to include in your report. Your notes will vary. Some will be very short, such as a date or the name of a city; some, like brief summaries of information, will be slightly longer; and some will be very lengthy, such as a passage copied word for word.

Material copied word for word must be enclosed in quotation marks to show that the words are not originally yours. Each quotation must include a footnote (a note at the bottom of the page indicating the source of the quotation) to let the reader know the title and other details about the reference source from which you copied the words.

Always remember that it is dishonest and unscrupulous to use someone else's phrases or sentences unless you use quotation marks and name the person who originally wrote or said those phrases or sentences. Using someone else's words as though they are your own is plagiarism, which is justification for a failing grade on a report. (See Chapter 7 for more on quotations and footnotes.)

In most cases, it will be easiest to write your notes on index cards. They are easy to carry around while you do research. Laying them out and changing their order can help you organize your thoughts when you begin to write your draft. Although you can use a computer to take notes, pulling them together when you write your draft will be a lot of work.

STEP-BY-STEP PLAN

When you are ready to take notes, follow these steps:

STEP 1

You will use your outline for this step. At the top of a 5- by 8-inch index card or 8½- by 11-inch sheet of paper, write down the first topic (or the file name for the topic) listed on your outline. Use a separate index card or piece of paper for every topic and subtopic on your outline.

STEP 2

Start at the beginning of the encyclopedia article about your topic and quickly look at the headings as you skim through the pages. When you come to a topic or subtopic listed on your outline, look carefully for the information you want.

STEP 3

If the article has useful information, write down the information you need for your bibliography before taking notes. This information is the author(s), title, place of publication, publisher, and copyright date. For electronic materials, you also write down the type of material (CD-ROM or on-line), the vendor or publisher, and the publication date or the date of access for on-line databases. Use a 3- by 5-inch index card and write the information in the correct order. (See the examples in Appendix B.)

STEP 4

Put a letter code in the upper right-hand corner of the bibliography card. The first source you use will be coded "A," the second "B," and so on. Because you will use the same information in your footnotes, using the codes means that you only have to write the complete information down once.

STEP 5

When you find useful information about the topic or subtopic, write it on a 5- by 8-inch index card with the corresponding heading.

E X A M P L E S :

Lee Harvey Oswald

Formative Years
- Born 10/18/39 in New Orleans
- Father died 2 months before 10/18/39
- Placed in orphanage when 3 yrs. old
- Taken out of orphanage when 4 to move to Dallas with mother
- Mother remarried and later divorced
- Between grades 1–6 moved to Covington, Louisiana, Fort Worth, Texas, and New York City
- Declining report card grades over the years
- Chronic truant when 13 and 14
- Diagnosed as emotionally disturbed
- Above average intelligence
- Fantasized about being a powerful person and about hurting people

---

JFK's Intimacy with Friends
of Underworld Figures

Marilyn Monroe
- Blonde movie star
- Introduced to JFK by Frank Sinatra
- Introduced to underworld figures, enemies of the Kennedys, by Sinatra
- Underworld figures secretly tape recorded trysts with JFK
- Tapes expected to pressure JFK and brother Robert to decrease or drop pursuit of organized crime
- Tapes not used; assassination achieved desired results

If you copy phrases or sentences word for word, be certain to copy the words and punctuation exactly as they appear. Put quotation marks before the first word and after the last word you copy and write down the code letter from the bibliography card for that reference source and the page number(s) on which the words appeared.

SAMPLE BIBLIOGRAPHY CARD

A

Summers, Anthony. <u>Conspiracy</u>.
    New York: McGraw-Hill, 1980.

SAMPLE NOTE CARD

Organized Crime – Marcello

- Marcello ". . . spoke of meting out Mafia justice to the Kennedys." A Pg. 337
- Marcello had contact with Jack Ruby
- Deported in 1961
- Later reentered USA illegally

SAMPLE BIBLIOGRAPHY CARD

B

Blakey, Robert G., and Richard N. Billings,
   The Plot to Kill the President. New York:
   Time Books, 1981.

SAMPLE NOTE CARD

Organized Crime – Jack Ruby
- Ruby shot and killed Lee Harvey Oswald 11/24/63
- "The murder of Oswald by Jack Ruby had all the earmarks
  of an organized-crime hit, an action to silence the assassin,
  so he could not reveal the conspiracy." B Pg. 339
- Owned a nightclub in Dallas

STEP 6

Repeat these steps for each source of information you use. Check
your notes to make sure that you have information that covers
all the topics and subtopics in your outline.

CHAPTER 6
CONDUCTING
AN INTERVIEW

An interview enables you to obtain firsthand information not available in books or other reference sources, and it adds a special touch to your research report.

FINDING INTERVIEW SUBJECTS

Locate people to interview by calling professional or trade organizations related to your topic. Many such organizations keep a list of experts in their field who are available for interviews. The *Encyclopedia of Associations* is a good source of such organizations. A librarian can also help you locate local experts.

The discussion groups of on-line services can be one of the best places to locate people to interview. These groups are called "forums" on CompuServe and "clubs and interests" on America Online. On other services, they might be called "roundtables" or "special interest groups." There are groups for every topic on which you might choose to write a report.

Find a group interested in your topic by looking at the service's list of groups and then reviewing the current messages posted in that group. When you find an appropriate group, post a brief message describing your topic and the kind of person you would like to interview. Be sure to consider carefully the qualifications of the people who respond before scheduling an interview.

When you write or type the questions for the interview, leave spaces for the responses. This will not only save you time when conducting the interview but will also simplify your note taking.

Establish a friendly atmosphere at the outset of the interview. Always look directly at the person when asking questions and when listening to responses.

If you are conducting the interview on-line, you have two choices, depending on the features of the on-line service you are using. You can send a message with your questions and wait for the response, or you can ask the questions in a "chat," a feature that works like a telephone conversation in that you type a question that appears simultaneously on your interviewee's screen and he or she types an answer that appears simultaneously on your screen. You can save either kind of response on the computer to print later or incorporate directly into your draft.

STEP-BY-STEP PLAN

The following steps will help you set up and conduct interviews.

STEP 1

Write a letter or send an electronic mail message to request an interview. See the samples on pages 49 and 50.

- Tell who you are and why you are requesting the interview.
- Suggest a date and time.
- Indicate that you will telephone one week from the date of the letter to firm up plans for the interview.

When you call to firm up plans, schedule the interview well in advance of the date the research report is due. If you are meeting in person, suggest as the meeting place the interviewee's office. For interviews with friends or relatives of a person about whom you are writing, mention that you would enjoy seeing pictures and mementos and ask that they bring such items to the interview.

STEP 2

Prepare a list of questions. Begin by asking yourself, WHO, WHAT, WHEN, WHERE, WHY, and HOW? If the person you are interviewing is acquainted with the subject of your report, you might compile questions such as the following:

- How did you meet the person?
- When and where did you meet the person?
- Who were the person's closest friends?
- Did you ever think the person would become famous? Why?
- How well did you know the person?
- What activities did you do together?
- Did you know the person's family?
- What was the person like before he or she became famous?

- How did the person change after becoming famous?
- What is your most striking memory of this person?
- Did the person influence you in any way? How?

Avoid questions that elicit one-word responses.

STEP 3

Practice the interview. Try out your questions on a family member or other adult. Add, delete, or rephrase the questions as necessary.

STEP 4

Conduct the interview. Begin by introducing yourself and thanking the person for agreeing to the interview. If you are meeting in person, shake hands. Then proceed with your questions.

STEP 5

Take concise notes. Write down only the important points. If you have a tape recorder, bring it to the interview and ask for permission to use it.

STEP 6

End the interview within the agreed-upon time frame. Thank the person for the interview and ask permission to call at a later date should you have additional questions.

STEP 7

Write a thank-you note. See the sample on page 51.

2425 Douglas Street
McLean, Virginia 22102
November 1, 1995

Mr. Benjamin Jackson
33 Corn Tassel Road
Danbury, CT 06810

Dear Mr. Jackson,

As a requirement for my ninth-grade English class, I am writing a report on Elvis Presley's influence upon musicians of the 1970s and 1980s. My neighbor, Mr. John Smith, a business associate of yours, told me that you went to school with Elvis, and he suggested that I get in touch with you. Therefore, I am writing to request an interview to obtain information regarding your memories of Elvis.

I will telephone you within the next few days to see if a thirty-minute meeting one day next week is convenient for you.

Thank you for the attention and consideration you give this request. I look forward to meeting you.

Sincerely,

Susan Tong

SUBJECT: Did Elvis Influence You?
FROM: suetong

My name is Susan and I am writing a research paper for my high school history class on the influence of Elvis Presley's music upon musicians of the 1970s and 1980s. I would like to interview musicians who knew Elvis Presley or whose musical style was heavily influenced by him. Can you point me to any good sources? I will give full credit for any information provided.

Thanks in advance,

Susan

2425 Douglas Street
McLean, Virginia 22102
November 10, 1995

Mr. Benjamin Jackson
33 Corn Tassel Road
Danbury, CT 06810

Dear Mr. Jackson,

Thank you for meeting with me this afternoon. I enjoyed hearing about your friendship with Elvis Presley, and I am grateful to you for sharing your many happy memories of that friendship.

The information you gave me will add special interest to my research report.

Sincerely,

Susan Tong

CHAPTER 7 USING QUOTATIONS AND FOOTNOTES

When you include in your writing phrases and sentences someone else has said or written, you are quoting that person and you must use quotation marks to show that the words are not originally yours. Use quotations to support your point of view, to show what experts are saying, or to show the results of a study or survey.

Along with each quotation you must use a footnote to tell the reader the source from which the quotation was taken. Always remember that using someone else's words without footnoting them is plagiarism.

Your teacher may allow you to use endnotes, which are footnotes that appear at the end of your report. Word processing programs let you create and number both footnotes and endnotes automatically. In either case, using the bibliography card codes and page numbers that you wrote on your note cards will help you make sure that you include the correct information.

STEP-BY-STEP PLAN

The following directions will guide you when preparing your footnotes.

STEP 1

Number your quotations in order beginning with the numeral 1. If you are using a typewriter, place each numeral ½ space above the end of each quotation. Begin each footnote with the same numeral as the corresponding quotation. If you are using a computer, use the footnote function to insert the appropriate numbers automatically.

STEP 2

Put every footnote at the bottom of the page on which the quotation appears. Indent the first line of every footnote five spaces. Type each footnote numeral before and a half space above the footnote information. The footnote function in a word processing program automatically places the footnote at the bottom of the page for you.

STEP 3

Take the information for your footnotes from your bibliography cards. Write or type the required information, punctuation, and page numbers in the order shown in the examples of footnotes for books, periodicals, and encyclopedias that follow.

EXAMPLES:

BOOK

[1]Jim Bishop, *The Day Kennedy Was Shot* (New York: Funk & Wagnalls, 1968), 23.

PERIODICAL

[2]Howard Kohn, "Execution for the Witnesses," *Rolling Stone*, 2 June 1977: 42–44.

ENCYCLOPEDIA

[3]Eric Sevareid, "Kennedy, John Fitzgerald," *World Book Encyclopedia*, 1992 ed.

If you use quotations from other sources, such as newspapers, pamphlets, interviews, CD-ROMs, or databases, see Appendix B for the correct footnote form. If you type your bibliography on a word processor, you can copy and paste the footnotes to compile your bibliography. This avoids retyping the same information, but you will have to change the format slightly. (See the examples in Appendix B.)

CHAPTER 8
WRITING
THE DRAFT

It is virtually impossible to write an error-free report that will satisfy you after the first writing. Therefore, the first copy of your report is considered a draft, a copy that is not in its final form. It is a copy that you will proofread for errors and edit in order to improve what you initially wrote. You may, as most writers do, write several drafts before deciding that your report is both well written and interesting. The object is to write a report that others will want to read from beginning to end.

HELPFUL HINTS

Style hints for report writing are beyond the scope of this book, but there are many fine books on the topic. The most common writing mistakes can be easily avoided, however. Use simple, straightforward wording. Avoid contractions, abbreviations, and slang. Avoid using the word "I." For example, do not write, "I think Elvis Presley influenced the music of others." Instead write, "Elvis Presley influenced the music of others."

If you are going to use a word processor to produce the final copy of your report, it is advisable to type your draft on the computer as well. It will be much easier to edit and revise. You can handwrite your draft and then type it into the computer, or you can type your draft straight onto the computer.

Be sure you give the computer file a name that you can recognize easily. If you use more than one file, a good idea is to use the roman numerals and letters of major topics from your outline. You can also use the document summary function, if the software has one, to identify the file more specifically.

STEP-BY-STEP PLAN

Follow these steps as you write your draft:

STEP 1

Your outline and notes provide the framework for your draft. Organize your note cards in the order in which each topic appears on your outline.

STEP 2

Reread your notes.

STEP 3

Take time to organize your thoughts and ideas.

STEP 4

When you begin to write, number and date each page of your draft copies. If you are writing directly on a computer, use the page numbering and automatic dating functions to do this.

STEP 5

Leave space between the lines on which you write so you can easily make changes as you reread your draft. Write on only one side of the paper. When using a word processor, use the line spacing function to double space your draft.

STEP 6

Include quotations to add strength to the points you want to make.

STEP 7

In your draft, write the bibliography card code of the book and the pages from which each quotation was taken. These notes will help you when you are ready to type the footnotes in your final copy.

THE BODY OF THE REPORT

As you write your draft you will concentrate on the title, introduction, body, and conclusion of your report. Often it is easier to write the body of the report first and then work on the wording of the title, introduction, and conclusion.

The body of a report contains the information you gathered as you did your research. Write the body to present this information in an organized and logical way. Weave the information and quotations you have collected into interesting sentences and paragraphs incorporating quotations into the text.

You will find it beneficial to consult books on expository writing such as: *Write Papers* by Robin Fry (Carter Press, 2nd ed., 1994), *The Writer's Handbook* by John B. Karls and Ronald Szymanski (National Textbook Co., 2nd ed., 1994), *On Writing Well: An Informal Guide to Writing Nonfiction* by William Zinsser (Harper Perennial, 5th ed., 1994), and *The New Oxford Guide to Writing* by Thomas S. Kane (Oxford University Press, 1988).

THE TITLE, THE INTRODUCTION, AND THE CONCLUSION

The title and the introductory paragraph form the cornerstone of your report. They should not only introduce the subject of your report but also arouse the interest of the reader. From the outset, you want to grab the reader's attention and compel him or her to read your report from beginning to end. Thus, it is imperative that you concentrate your effort and energy on producing an eye-catching title and a top-notch opening paragraph.

The concluding paragraph summarizes what you have learned and states the conclusions you have drawn based upon your research. The conclusion is very important. Use it to emphasize the main point(s) you have made and want to leave in the mind of the reader.

The following are examples of good titles, introductions, and conclusions.

CAN THE USE OF CHEMICAL AND BIOLOGICAL WEAPONS EVER BE JUSTIFIED?

The use of chemical and biological weapons is abhorrent to most people. However, there are those who would point out that the use of such weapons is no more reprehensible than the employment of nuclear arms, since the use of any one of these weapons would result in the horrific deaths of innocent civilians. This report will address the capabilities of nuclear, chemical, and biological weapons, their short- and long-term effects upon plant and animal life, and their impact upon the environment in order to determine whether or not the use of chemical and biological weapons is justifiable.

NOBLE CAUSE! IGNOBLE METHODS?

Since the dawn of civilization, human beings have worn fur because it was easily accessible and provided the necessary warmth for survival. To this day, men and women love the luxury, beauty, and warmth of fur. Now that fur is no longer necessary for survival, there are those people, specifically the animal-rights activists, who strongly believe that owning fur is unwarranted and reprehensible. While their cause is a noble one, the methods they use to influence public opinion are the subject of considerable debate and controversy.

ELVIS PRESLEY LIVES ON IN THE MUSIC OF OTHERS

Elvis Presley's sultry-eyed handsome face, unique vocal and instrumental style, and risqué pelvic moves mesmerized American youth in the 1950s and 1960s. To this day the influence of his style can be heard in the top hits and seen in the carefully choreographed moves of the most popular recording artists. This report will chronicle the effects that Elvis had on the music and performances of many of those who rose to fame from the sixties through the eighties.

SAMPLE CONCLUSIONS

(Can the Use of Chemical and Biological Weapons Ever be Justified?)

One must be realistic and face the fact that as long as human life exists on this planet people will undoubtedly have weapons to protect themselves. Therefore, it is not the type of weapon used but the ultimate destruction caused by weapons that is of concern. Based upon the information presented in this report regarding the loss of life and impact upon the environment, the use of biological and chemical weapons would be less devastating than the use of nuclear weapons. While the former would result in loss of life and damage to the environment, the latter would result in total obliteration of everything within a frighteningly large radius. Therefore, in this context, the use of chemical and biological weapons can be justified.

(Noble Cause! Ignoble Methods?)

There is little question that animal-rights activists have raised the consciousness of the public regarding the killing of animals for their fur. What does come into question are the methods they use in their zeal to protect animals. Verbal and physical confrontations directed toward people wearing fur have had a negative impact upon a worthy cause. Therefore, animal-rights activists must change their tactics and present their viewpoint in a more rational and socially acceptable manner. Only then will they make significant progress in protecting animals from being slaughtered for fur used solely for extravagant ornamentation rather than for survival.

(Elvis Presley Lives On in the Music of Others)

Elvis Presley's hip-swiveling gyrations, flamboyant clothing, and unique rendition of blues and country music launched the era of rock 'n' roll. The Presley phenomenon has influenced singers and musicians from the early sixties to the present day. Superstars such as the Beatles, Elton John, Bruce Springsteen, and Michael Jackson are among the most successful entertainers who have been influenced by Presley.

Musicians have identified with the lyrics of Presley's music, which describe the emotional highs and lows and rebellious nature of youth. Presley became the catalyst that freed musicians to express their own feelings and concerns in their music. Elvis Presley steered the course of music in a new direction, thus influencing generations of musicians.

CHAPTER 9 PROOFREADING, EDITING, AND REVISING

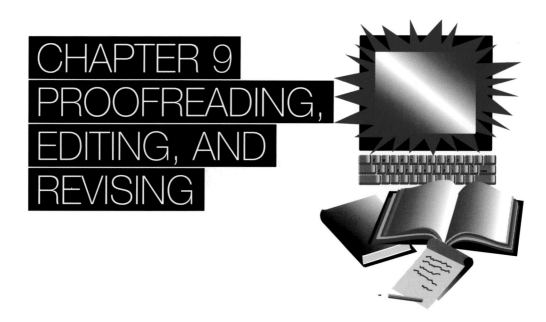

You proofread and edit to find and correct mistakes in content, spelling, grammar, and punctuation. You revise to improve the quality and content of your writing.

You will probably revise parts of your paper several times before you are satisfied with the final result. Careful proofreading, editing, and improved revisions can often mean the difference between a good report and an excellent one.

USING THE COMPUTER

If you typed your draft on a word processor, you should print it out for this step. It is usually easier to make corrections and notes about revisions on paper and then enter the changes on the computer. If you find material you want to take out, it is a good idea to save it as a separate file with a different name in case you change your mind.

If you are producing your paper with a word processor, you may be able to use program functions that make proofreading and editing easier. Most word-processing programs have a function that checks spelling, and many have a thesaurus function. Some have a grammar check function, which is also available in separate software programs.

These word-processing functions can simplify your editing and proofreading, but they cannot do the whole job for you. Be aware that spelling checks do not correct your spelling automatically. They compare what you have typed with the dictionary that comes with the software and highlight only those words that do not match anything in the dictionary. Some offer you choices of how to spell the word, some do not; in either case, you must choose the correct spelling. They will not catch mix-ups like "to" for "too"; this is why you must proofread your paper yourself. The same is true of grammar check functions; they only compare what you have typed with a particular set of guidelines. You must still decide what changes to make.

STEP-BY-STEP PLAN

Allow enough time after writing your draft to take a break from looking at your paper. This will make it easier for you to spot errors in what you have written. Follow these steps to ensure a thorough job of proofreading, editing, and revising:

STEP 1

Reread your report carefully, focusing on content. Have you conveyed information clearly to the reader? Does your paper make sense?

STEP 2

Reread your report for spelling mistakes, and use your dictionary when necessary. Consult a thesaurus to find alternatives for overused words.

STEP 3

Check for grammatical errors and mistakes in punctuation, using as a resource your English textbook or a reference book such as *The Elements of Style* (Strunk and White, 3rd ed., Macmillan, 1979). Another resource is *The Chicago Manual of Style* (14th ed., University of Chicago Press, 1993), which is regarded by many as the most comprehensive reference book on writing. Other books containing grammar and punctuation rules are available in public libraries.

STEP 4

Read your report out loud to hear how the words sound and to find mistakes in your writing that you might otherwise overlook.

STEP 5

Reread again and revise the sentences and paragraphs that would sound and read better if worded differently. Sometimes this is simply a matter of changing the order of sentences in a paragraph.

STEP 6

Have a friend or relative read your final revision, making suggestions and corrections where appropriate.

STEP 7

Now that you have finished proofreading, editing, and revising your report, you are ready to prepare your final copy. Proofread this copy to make sure that you have made all your changes correctly.

CHAPTER 10
USING
GRAPHICS

Graphics such as tables, charts, graphs, and illustrations such as maps help convey statistical information, clarify a subject, and reinforce a point. Use tables to display numerical information. Use line graphs and bar charts to display trends. Use pie charts to show proportions. Use maps when geographic location is important to your topic.

Check to see if your teacher has any requirements for the use of graphics. Be sure every graphic you use is simple and easy to interpret. Use a graphic only when it helps to visually convey and reinforce the information in your report.

Many computer programs with clip art (illustrations and symbols) are available. If you are using a computer, make sure you know how to use the graphics software before you decide to include graphics in your report. No generalizations can be made about how to use them. Consult a manual for directions. Remember that graphics copied from other sources should be credited in a footnote.

STEP-BY-STEP PLAN

The following steps will help you incorporate graphics in your report.

STEP 1

Decide whether you need to use a graphic. A rule of thumb is to use a graphic only if it will clarify or reinforce what you have written.

STEP 2

Decide which type of graphic is best for the information you want to convey.

STEP 3

Compile the information for your table, create your chart or graph, or locate an illustration.

STEP 4

Type a title above every table and below every other type of graphic to let the reader know what the graphic depicts.

STEP 5

For every graphic in your report, include a matching "call-out" in your text; for example, "See Table 1."

STEP 6

Number the tables, charts, graphs, illustrations, and maps in the order they appear in your report.

CHAPTER 11
COMPILING A
BIBLIOGRAPHY

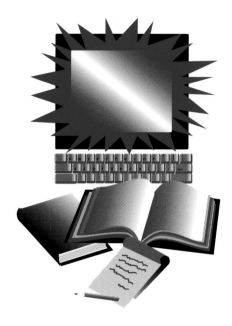

You include a bibliography at the end of your research report to show the sources you used to gather information for the report.

Make sure that you have written down all the information about a source on the bibliography card for that source. It can be very time consuming to go back to the library and find a source again because you forgot to write down an author's first name or the place where it was published.

Some word-processing programs allow you to open the internal file where your footnotes are stored. In these programs, to avoid retyping, you can copy all your footnotes and paste them into your bibliography. You will have to change the order in which the information appears in each entry.

STEP-BY-STEP PLAN

The following steps will help you compile your bibliography.

STEP 1

Arrange your bibliography cards in alphabetical order according to the author's last name. If an author's name is not given, alphabetize by the title of the source. If you have already entered the information in a computer file, you may be able to use the word processor's "Sort" function to alphabetize the entries. Check the program's "Help" function or your manual to learn how to use this function. Not all word-processing programs have this function.

STEP 2

Before typing the bibliography, refer to Appendix B for the correct bibliographic form for different types of references. (Examples are given for books with one author, books with two authors, and encyclopedia articles, as well as CD-ROMs and on-line databases.) Type the information for each entry in the correct order when using a computer, so you do not have to go back later to rearrange it.

STEP 3

Center the title, BIBLIOGRAPHY, at the top of the page.

STEP 4

Begin the first line of each entry at the left margin. Indent succeeding lines five spaces. On both typewriters and computers, it is best to set a tab for this purpose. Single space within entries and double space between entries.

EXAMPLES:

BOOK

Bishop, Jim. *The Day Kennedy Was Shot.* New York: Funk & Wagnalls, 1968.

PERIODICAL

Kohn, Howard. "Execution for the Witnesses." *Rolling Stone.* June 1977, 42–44.

ENCYCLOPEDIA

Sevareid, Eric. "Kennedy, John Fitzgerald." *World Book Encyclopedia.* 1992 ed.

CHAPTER 12 PRODUCING A FINAL REPORT

The final copy of your report can be handwritten unless your teacher specifies that it must be typewritten. A typed report is more visually attractive as well as easier to read. Because of these advantages, it is probably best that you use a typewriter or a word processor to prepare your final report whenever possible.

OPTIONS

If you use a word processor, you may be tempted to "dress up" your report with different typefaces or layouts. It is very easy to overdo this. A visually attractive and easy-to-read report has a clean, simple style. Avoid mixing typefaces and sizes or using lots of ruled lines and boxes. If your teacher has specified a format for the paper, follow it carefully; if not, use the guidelines given here. (A sample report is shown in Appendix C.)

Some word-processing programs come with "Templates," guides that contain codes for margins and spacing and sometimes formats for footnotes and chapter headings (in a function called "Styles"). If you use a template, make sure it matches your teacher's requirements.

To further add to the visual appeal of your report, you will want to bind it using an attractive cover. A graphic created from clip art or a draw program on your computer would be effective—or you might find an appropriate image to copy in the course of your research.

STEP-BY-STEP PLAN

Follow these steps and use the format shown in the sample report when typing your final copy:

STEP 1

Proofread your most recent draft one more time before producing your final copy.

STEP 2

Decide how you are going to bind your report and then allow for at least an inch margin on the left and right edges of every page. Remember to plan for the space that the binding requires. If, for example, you are going to bind your report along the left side, you will want to allow at least 1½ inches for the left margin (depending upon the width of the binding) so that the reader will see a 1-inch margin on the left and right edges of every page. Top and bottom margins of 1 to 1½ inches will give your report a neat and balanced appearance. If you are using a word processor, you only have to set the margins once.

STEP 3

Type or print out your paper on only one side of each sheet of paper. Double space all typing except for footnotes, bibliography entries, lengthy quotations, and any tables. Word-processing programs allow you to set the margins and line spacing using a function called "Page Setup," "Page Layout," or similar terms. When using graphics, make sure they appear after the call-out.

STEP 4

Type a title page with the title of your report as well as your name, the date, and the name of the course for which you wrote the report.

STEP 5

Type a table of contents on a separate page. If you are using a word-processing program, use the "Help" command or your manual to find out how to generate a table of contents. These functions are sometimes called "Indexing" or "Tables." They keep track of the right page numbers automatically.

STEP 6

Type the body of your report and number the pages as shown in the sample report in Appendix C. If you are using a word-processing program, use the "Pagination" or "Page Numbering" command to insert page numbers automatically.

STEP 7

On a separate page, type your bibliography. See Appendix B for specific details about the various types of entries.

STEP 8

Proofread your typed report and correct all errors.

STEP 9

Have someone else proofread your report. Correct any errors that person finds.

APPENDIX A
SOURCES OF
INFORMATION

Information for your reports can be found in general books, specific reference books, and a wide variety of other sources. This chapter is devoted to a broad overview of sources of information. These sources include materials in print form and electronic form. The bulk of most library resources are printed, but CD-ROM packages and on-line databases are now widely available. A majority of libraries are equipped with some CD-ROM materials, and many have some kind of access to on-line databases through consumer services like Prodigy and CompuServe or academic services like DIALOG.

These sources may not all be available in your library. A librarian can help you find sources similar to the ones listed here. You may also be able to access a consumer information service on a home computer. Remember that if it is difficult to locate information on your topic, you may need to choose a different topic. That is the purpose of your preliminary search for information.

GENERAL ENCYCLOPEDIAS

General encyclopedias are excellent sources of background information. In a few volumes they present pertinent facts and explanations of concepts in all branches of human knowledge.

Popular, reliable general encyclopedias include the following:

New Encyclopaedia Britannica. Chicago, Encyclopaedia Britannica, Inc.

Encyclopedia Americana. Danbury, Conn., Grolier.

World Book Encyclopedia. Chicago, Scott Fetzer.

Collier's Encyclopedia. New York, Macmillan.

Compton's Encyclopedia and Fact-Index. Chicago, Encyclopaedia Britannica, Inc.

Academic American Encyclopedia. Danbury, Conn., Grolier.

Articles in these encyclopedias are reviewed regularly and revised as needed on a continuing basis. Therefore, new editions come out almost every year.

Encyclopedias come in print and electronic form. Every library's reference center will have at least one of these encyclopedias on the shelves. Several are also available in CD-ROM packages, some of which come prepackaged with home computers. *Compton's* and the *Academic American* are available through the major commercial on-line services (such as America Online, CompuServe, Prodigy). The *Britannica* is available on the Internet.

SUBJECT ENCYCLOPEDIAS

Subject encyclopedias are specialized encyclopedias containing information about specific subjects such as music, science, and art. Following is a list of subject encyclopedias that your library might have in its collection:

Dictionary of American History. New York, Scribner's, 1976.

Articles in this dictionary cover political, economic, social, industrial, and cultural history.

Encyclopedia of Philosophy. New York, Macmillan, 1973.

This encyclopedia focuses on Eastern and Western philosophy and covers ancient, medieval, and modern philosophy.

International Encyclopedia of the Social Sciences. New York, Macmillan, 1977.

In this encyclopedia lengthy authoritative articles cover broad fields such as anthropology, economics, geography, history, law, political science, psychology, and sociology.

McGraw-Hill Encyclopedia of Science and Technology. New York, McGraw-Hill, 1987.

This encyclopedia covers all branches of science and technology. Information is kept current with the annual *McGraw-Hill Yearbook of Science and Technology*. An edition is available on CD-ROM (1992–).

The New Grove Dictionary of Music and Musicians. New York, Macmillan, 1980.

This encyclopedia contains articles about musical forms and concepts, composers, and musicians. This edition includes popular music and jazz.

ALMANACS AND YEARBOOKS

Basic, factual information found in general publications and encyclopedias can be brought up to date by the use of annual yearbooks and almanacs. Many of the leading encyclopedias publish their own annual supplements, which describe the events of the year just past and include the latest statistics needed to keep their general work current. Among these are the *Americana Annual, Britannica Book of the Year,* and *World Book Year Book.*

In addition to these supplementary volumes, there are numerous general almanacs and yearbooks that provide information and current statistics on a wide range of subjects. They can be used to answer a wide array of questions: How many nuclear power plants are there currently in the United States? Did Hemingway ever win the Nobel Prize for literature? Where are presidential libraries located? What are the Seven Wonders of the World? Articles may review the year's events in broad fields such as books, sports, theater, film, music, and so on. All provide statistics on social, industrial, political, financial, religious, educational, and other topics. They also contain factual information about countries and listings of popular items such as Nobel Prizes, sports records, famous historical events, etc.

Your library will have an almanac in the reference section; some almanacs are available on CD-ROM. Two popular almanacs include the *Information Please Almanac, Atlas and Yearbook* (New York, Simon and Schuster, 1947–), and the *World Almanac and Book of Facts* (New York, Pharos Books, 1968–).

STATISTICAL SOURCES

Although all almanacs include statistical information, the primary source for summaries of political, social, and economic statistics of the United States is the annual *Statistical Abstract of the United States* (Washington, U.S. Government Printing Office, 1879–). Tables generally cover statistics for the past 15 to 20 years but in some instances go back as far as 1789 or 1800. Sources of statistics are given for users who want additional information.

Three important supplements to the *Statistical Abstract* are the *County and City Data Book* (Washington, U.S. Government Printing Office, 1952– . Irregular), the *State and Metropolitan Area Data Book* (Washington, U.S. Government Printing Office, 1980–), and *Historical Statistics of the United States, Colonial Times to 1970* (Washington, U.S. Government Printing Office, 1975. 2 vols.). The *Data Books* provide census-based statistics for each state, county, and the larger cities in the United States. *Historical Statistics* includes comparative statistics of the type covered in the *Statistical Abstract*, going back to 1789.

Other sources of specialized statistics are available on CD-ROM and through on-line services (particularly CompuServe, Dow Jones News/Retrieval, and Prodigy). These sources typically cover subjects of interest to people involved in business and industry.

HANDBOOKS AND MANUALS

Handbooks contain miscellaneous facts with a common theme, such as the *Guinness Book of World Records* (New York, Sterling, 1955– . Annual) or Kane's *Famous First Facts* (4th ed. New York, Wilson, 1981).

Manuals such as car-repair manuals or books of etiquette tell how to do something. Manuals have been written to cover virtually all fields and serve as ready reference sources for the topics they cover. New ones appear constantly as popular needs and current areas of interest dictate.

MAGAZINE AND NEWSPAPER ARTICLES

The latest information about a topic of current interest will frequently be found in magazines and newspapers. There are a number of subject indexes to periodical articles. Few libraries will have all that are available, but each will have a selection of those that index the magazines and newspapers that the library receives.

Indexes are available in book form, on CD-ROM, and on-line through services such as GEnie and Dow Jones News/ Retrieval. Sometimes they are included in a library's on-line catalog. CD-ROM and on-line indexes are useful when you are searching for information about a very specific topic because you can search the index by limited, specific key words. On-line indexes are also helpful when you are looking for very recent articles for which a printed index has not yet been published.

Searches of indexes will produce a list of citations, but searches of full-text databases can produce a series of articles. It can be expensive to do on-line searches of these databases. If a library offers access to these databases, a librarian or an experienced researcher will usually do the search because he or she can do it quickly and efficiently.

MAGAZINE INDEXES

Since no single index covers all magazines, it is often necessary to identify those that index periodicals most closely related to a subject. The title of an index usually indicates the scope of material it covers, and each volume of an index lists at the beginning the magazines it includes.

The following is a brief selection of indexes that might be available in a local library. Many are available on-line (all the *Readers' Guide* indexes and *PAIS International*, for example); some are also available on CD-ROM (the *Business Periodicals Index*, for example). Some high school libraries have a CD-ROM index called TOM (1985–), which covers 140 magazines and includes the full text for 30 of them. Ask the librarian about the best ones to consult in a particular area of interest or research.

> *Readers' Guide to Periodical Literature*. New York, Wilson, 1900– . Semimonthly except July and August. Annual and cumulated volumes.
>
> This is the most familiar and readily available of the periodical indexes. It covers all major subjects and indexes U.S. magazines of a general and popular nature. It is available on CD-ROM (1983–). School and small public libraries may have the *Abridged Readers' Guide* (New York, Wilson, 1936–), which indexes fewer periodicals. Wilson also publishes a number of periodical indexes in specific subject areas: *Art Index, Book Review Index, Business Periodicals Index, Education Index, General Science Index, Humanities Index, Index to Legal Periodicals, Music Index, Social Science Index,* and the *Vertical File Index* (covering pamphlet material).
>
> *Magazine Index*. Los Altos, Calif., Information Access Corp., 1976– . Microfilm updated monthly.
>
> This index lists some 435 popular magazines (including those covered by *Readers' Guide*). The microfilm is viewed by users on a motorized, self-contained unit resembling a television set. Various versions of the index are available on CD-ROM (1980–).

Access: The Supplementary Index to Periodicals. Syracuse, N.Y., Gaylord, Burke, 1975– . Triennial with annual cumulation.

In this index the emphasis is on popular music, travel magazines, science fiction, and arts and crafts. Numerous regional and city magazines are also included.

PAIS Bulletin. New York, Public Affairs Information Service, 1915– . Biweekly with annual and five-year cumulations.

This is a subject index to current books, documents, pamphlets, reports of public and private agencies, and selected articles in English published throughout the world. It is especially useful for political science, government, legislation, economics, and sociology. A version is available on-line through various services.

NEWSPAPER INDEXES

There are no general printed indexes for newspaper articles comparable to those for magazines. However, since most newspapers publish stories of general, national, or international interest at approximately the same time, determining the date of an event will make it easier to locate these articles in any newspaper. Almanacs and yearbooks usually include a chronology of the previous year's major events.

An index to one newspaper, such as the *New York Times Index* (New York, Times, 1913– ; prior series, 1851–1912, New York, Bowker, 1966–), can serve as a date index to articles of general or national interest that appear in most large newspapers. The *New York Times Index* also gives brief synopses of articles, and often these will provide enough information to answer questions without the need to refer to the full story.

Many libraries also receive weekly issues of the world news digest *Facts on File* (New York, Facts on File, Inc., 1940–). This digest indexes news events and provides brief summaries of them. It is also available on CD-ROM and on-line through DIALOG, the Knowledge Index, and NEXIS, beginning with 1980.

Some printed newspaper indexes include the following:

Christian Science Monitor Index. Wooster, Ohio, Bell and Howell, 1960– . Monthly.

This contains retrospective indexing to 1950 as well as an index to Eastern, Western, and Midwestern editions of the *Monitor.*

Index to the Times. London, The Times, 1906– . Monthly since 1977. (The title varies.)

This indexes articles appearing in the English newspaper and its Literary, Education and Higher Educational supplements. Brief abstracts were added in 1977.

Newspaper Index. Wooster, Ohio, Bell and Howell, 1972– . Monthly.

This comprises separate indexes to six regionally important newspapers: *Houston Post, San Francisco Chronicle, Chicago Tribune, Los Angeles Times, New Orleans Times–Picayune,* and *Washington Post.*

Wall Street Journal Index. Princeton, N.J., Dow Jones, 1958– . Monthly with annual cumulations.

This indexes and briefly summarizes the corporate and general news items that appear in the *Wall Street Journal.*

Newsbank. NewsBank, 1980– . Monthly.

This CD-ROM index covers articles from 450 newspapers. It is also available in print. Copies of the articles listed in the index can be viewed on microfiche.

Newspapers are one source that can be easier to search on-line than in print. Indexes to major newspapers such as *The New York Times*, *The Wall Street Journal*, and *The Christian Science Monitor* are available on CD-ROM and in on-line databases. Both indexes and databases containing the full text of major newspaper articles are maintained by a variety of on-line services, such as NEXIS, DIALOG, and DataTimes. The most comprehensive newspaper databases are found in DIALOG Information Retrieval Service (accessible through CompuServe and GEnie and on the Internet) and Dow Jones News/Retrieval. Consumer on-line services such as CompuServe offer smaller databases. Check with a librarian to see which ones your library carries.

Databases from services such as NEXIS, DIALOG, and Data-Times provide the only indexing to articles in the local press. For local news items, many libraries maintain their own clipping files and newspaper indexes. The directory *Newspaper Indexes: A Location and Subject Guide for Researchers* (Metuchen, N. J., Scarecrow, 1977–1982. 3 vols.), tells which libraries index what newspapers and the years covered. In some cases, however, it may be necessary to write or call the newspapers themselves. Addresses and telephone numbers of newspapers throughout the country are readily available in a variety of references:

Gale Directory of Publications and Broadcast Media. Detroit, Gale Research, 1990– . Annual.

This directory provides an annual list of American newspapers, periodicals, and television and radio stations. It gives the addresses and telephone numbers, character or politics, subscription rate, circulation figures, and names of editors and publishers. It is available in print and on CD-ROM.

Editor and Publisher International Yearbook. New York, Editor and Publisher, 1920– . Annual.

This is an annual resource for American and Canadian daily newspapers, giving addresses, telephone numbers, circulation rates, executive personnel, and departmental managers and editors. It also lists weekly and daily newspapers from countries around the world and provides other information of special interest to journalists and newspaper publishers.

BIOGRAPHICAL INDEXES

These indexes do not provide biographical data but instead tell where the particular book or periodical in which information about a person may be found. These indexes can save extensive search time. Some major biographical indexes include the following:

Biography and Genealogy Master Index. 2d ed. Detroit, Gale Research, 1980. 8 vols. Supplements, 1981–84. Annual updates, 1985– .

This indexes current biographical dictionaries and directories in all fields, including art, architecture, music, the theater, athletics, education, government, law, the military, philosophy, religion, applied and social sciences, and others. Indexes since 1993 are available on micro-fiche (called BIO-BASE), on CD-ROM, and on-line through DIALOG.

Other indexes by the same publisher are: *Artists Biographies Master Index, Author Biographies Master Index, Journalist Biographies Master Index*, and *Performing Arts Biography Master Index*.

Biography Index. New York, Wilson, 1947– . Quarterly with annual and three-year cumulations.

This indexes biographical articles appearing in books and magazines (excluding biographical dictionaries). The index itself gives dates and the profession of individuals and their nationality if other than American. It is available on CD-ROM and on-line through the Wilsonline and FirstSearch services (1984–).

Marquis Who's Who Publications: Index to All Books. Chicago, Marquis, 1974– . Annual.

This indexes the names of all persons included in current world, national, regional, and other editions of Marquis *Who's Who* publications and the latest *Who Was Who in America*.

New York Times Obituaries Index. New York, Times, 1970– . Irregular.

News stories are indexed as well as obituaries that have appeared in the *New York Times* since 1958. Included are not just Americans but almost every prominent world figure who died during the years covered.

BIOGRAPHICAL DICTIONARIES OR DIRECTORIES

Biographical dictionaries or directories contain factual information about the individuals included in them. Many give only a brief outline of the person's life, the familiar "who's who" paragraph; others, such as *Current Biography* or the *Dictionary of American Biography*, contain entries that are often quite extensive and detailed.

To decide which biographical dictionary is needed, determine first whether the person is living or dead, the person's nationality, and the person's profession or occupation. A selection of some of the more popular biographical reference works available in print and electronic form is described. A librarian will be able to recommend others.

American Men and Women of Science: Physical and Biological Sciences. New York, Bowker, 1906– . Triennial.

This contains biographies of North American scientists representing all the biological and physical sciences, as well as computer science, engineering, and mathematics. It is available on-line through various services.

Contemporary Authors. Detroit, Gale Research, 1962– . Semiannual.

This includes lengthy biographical sketches of writers in many fields (humanities, social sciences, sciences). Mostly English-language writers, with some foreign writers, are represented. A complete bibliography is given for each author.

Current Biography. New York, Wilson, 1940– . Monthly except August with annual cumulations.

This contains articles on individuals in the news, including a photograph of each and citations to other articles.

Dictionary of American Biography. New York, Scribner's, 1928–37. 20 vols. and index. Supplements.

This includes scholarly articles on historically prominent Americans and bibliographical citations for biographies on each.

Who's Who. London, Black; New York, St. Martin's, 1849–1990. Annual.

This was the first great "who's who" listing people of distinction in all fields in the Commonwealth nations as well as Great Britain. Almost every major country publishes its own "who's who."

Who's Who Among Black Americans. Northbrook, Ill., Who's Who Among Black Americans, Inc., 1975/76– . Irregular.

It contains biographies of prominent blacks in all areas of achievement.

Who's Who in America. Chicago, Marquis, 1899– . 2 vols. Biennial.

This includes Americans, both men and women, of significant achievement in government, industry, education, religion, and other fields. It is available on CD-ROM and on-line through CompuServe, DIALOG, and the Knowledge Index.

Marquis also publishes four regional volumes for specific areas of the United States (*Who's Who in the East, Who's Who in the Midwest, Who's Who in the South and Southwest,* and *Who's Who in the West*); a retrospective series *Who*

Was Who in America; an international *Who's Who in the World*; and numerous directories by specific occupation or group. These last include: *Who's Who in American Law, Who's Who in Finance and Industry, Who's Who in Government,* and *Who's Who of American Women.*

Who's Who in American Art. New York, Bowker, 1935– . Irregular.

This contains brief biographies of painters, sculptors, graphic artists, craftsmen, historians, critics, editors, educators, lecturers, etc.

Who's Who in American Politics. New York, Bowker, 1967/68– . Biennial.

This contains biographies of U.S. political leaders ranging from the president to local figures.

DIRECTORIES OF ORGANIZATIONS, INSTITUTIONS, AND CORPORATIONS

Frequently, contacting organizations formed around a specific interest or objective can produce information related to that interest more efficiently and quickly than conducting research in books or periodicals. This is particularly true in scientific, industrial, and other rapidly changing fields. These organizations can provide the names of people to interview. Numerous print directories are available to help identify these organizations. Many such organizations can also be found through on-line services in features called discussion groups, which are also good sources for names of experts to interview.

The standard directory of national and international membership organizations is the *Encyclopedia of Associations* (Detroit, Gale Research, 1964– . 4 vols. Annual), supplemented by the serial *New Associations*. It is possible to look up an organization by name or keyword and find a brief description of the group in addition to a current address and telephone number. Associations in all subject areas are covered. Volumes 1–3 focus on U.S. nonprofit groups; volume 4, which first appeared in 1986, covers international organizations. A seven-volume separate set covers regional, state, and local organizations. It is also available on CD-ROM and on-line through DIALOG.

If a directory in a more specific area than the subjects covered by the *Encyclopedia of Associations* is required, a librarian can offer suggestions. Directories can also be found in the library's catalog; look for the subject division DIRECTORIES following the main subject. Another alternative is to consult *Guide to American Directories* (New York, McGraw-Hill, 1954–) or *Directories in Print* (Detroit, Gale Research, 1980–). These describe United States and some foreign directories arranged by subject, technical/mercantile, scientific, and professional headings.

Some directories of different types of organizations, institutions, and corporations include:

American Universities and Colleges. Washington, American Council on Education, 1928– . Quadrennial.

For institutions accredited by the Council, this directory gives history, resources, staff analysis, student enrollment, degrees granted, professional schools, and other information.

Conservation Directory. Washington, National Wildlife Federation, 1900– . Annual.

It lists U.S., Canadian, and other international organizations and agencies concerned with natural resource use and management.

Directory of Historical Agencies in North America. Nashville, American Association for State and Local History, 1956– . Irregular.

This directory gives names and addresses of agencies, associations, libraries, museums, and other groups interested in state and local history.

Encyclopedic Directory of Ethnic Organizations in the United States. Littleton, Colo., Libraries Unlimited, 1975.

This directory describes causes and activities of major American ethnic groups and their associations.

Foundation Directory. New York, Foundation Center, 1960– . Biennial.

This contains information about major private American foundations and is useful for fundraisers who need some background data before approaching an institution for project support.

Literary Market Place. New York, Bowker, 1940– . Annual.

This directory of the book publishing industry includes listings of U.S. and Canadian publishers; foreign publishers with U.S. offices; book clubs; literary, illustration, and lecture agents; associations, organizations and foundations; book trade events, conferences, and courses; and radio and television programs featuring books.

Official Museum Directory. American Association of Museums, 1971– . Annual.

This describes museums of all types—art, history, science—and gives their addresses, sponsors, directors, publications, hours of opening, and so forth.

Poor's Register of Corporations, Directors and Executives. New York, Standard and Poor's, 1928– . Annual. 3 vols.

This lists American and Canadian corporations and gives the names of officers, types of products, and number of employees, including biographies of officers and executives.

Thomas' Register of American Manufacturers. New York, Thomas, 1905– . Annual. 20+ vols.

This lists, for manufactured products and services, "all known manufacturers and sources," including indexes of trademarks, products and services, and manufacturers' catalogs. It is also available on CD-ROM and on-line through DIALOG.

PUBLICATIONS OF THE FEDERAL GOVERNMENT

Publications of the federal government, most of them issued by the U.S. Government Printing Office (GPO), provide a wealth of information not only about the operations of Congress and the executive departments of the federal government but also about many aspects of the U.S. economy and social structure. The GPO distributes material concerning farming, homemaking, education, transportation, small business, housing, crime, wildlife, and numerous other topics.

So that the public may know what documents are available, the GPO publishes an index, the *Monthly Catalog of United States Government Publications* (Washington, U.S. Government Printing Office, 1895–). Publications are arranged by the issuing agency and then indexed in turn by subject, author, title, and series/report number. Cumulative indexes come out twice a year.

The *Monthly Catalog* is also available from a variety of CD-ROM producers:

Government Documents Catalog Service. Auto-Graphics, Inc., 1976– .

This version of the complete *Monthly Catalog* lets you do complex searches and download records.

G.P.O. on Silverplatter. SilverPlatter Information, Inc., 1976– .

This disk contains citations on books, reports, studies, serials, maps from the *Monthly Catalog*.

Government Publications Index on Infotrac. Information Access, 1976– .

This index covers public documents of the government since 1976.

The GPO also offers a catalog of all publications that it currently has for sale. The *Publications Reference File* is available on microfiche and magnetic tape; it can also be searched on-line through DIALOG.

Four times a year, the GPO also issues *U.S. Government Books* which contains approximately 1,000 descriptions of the most popular publications available for sale from the GPO. It is free to subscribers. This publication was first issued in 1982 and replaced *Selected U.S. Government Publications*. To be added to the distribution list, you may write to:

Superintendent of Documents
U.S. Government Printing Office
Washington, D.C. 20402

Also introduced in 1982 was the bimonthly catalog *New Books*, an unannotated listing of all new titles introduced for sale over the preceding two months. It is also available free to subscribers of the *Monthly Catalog*.

In addition to the *Monthly Catalog, U.S. Government Books*, and *New Books*, the GPO also prepares some 250 bibliographies of its publications on various general topics such as Congress, consumer information, foreign relations of the United States, oil spills and ocean dumping, social welfare and services, Spanish publications, and so forth. Write to the GPO in Washington, D.C., indicating the topics of interest, and they will send the appropriate bibliographies without charge. You may request a copy of their *Subject Bibliography Index,* which names all those that are available.

Another federal agency, the General Services Administration, also distributes government pamphlets selected specifically for their usefulness to consumers. These cover topics such as how to fix a car and how to stay fit. A quarterly *Consumer Information Catalog* describes items available. To obtain a free copy of the catalog, write:

Consumer Information Center
Pueblo, Colorado 81009

If these publications are not available at a public or research library, they may be available at a government depository library. Over 1,300 public and research libraries throughout the country have been designated as depositories and automatically receive numerous government publications. A librarian can direct you to the nearest U.S. government depository library.

Publications can also be purchased directly from the Superintendent of Documents in Washington, D.C. Prices of items that are for sale are given in the publication lists. All orders must be accompanied by full payment or can be charged using commercial credit cards.

Finally, the GPO currently operates some 25 bookstores in major cities throughout the country. Six of the stores are located in the metropolitan Washington, D.C., area. Others are located in Atlanta, Birmingham, Boston, Chicago, Cleveland, Columbus, Dallas, Denver, Detroit, Houston, Jacksonville, Kansas City, Los Angeles, Milwaukee, New York, Philadelphia, Pueblo, San Francisco, and Seattle. Addresses can be found in the white pages of a local telephone directory under the listing "U.S. Government."

FEDERAL AGENCIES AND PROGRAMS

If material is needed on how the federal government is organized, what federal programs are available to help with a community project, what federal funds have been distributed to a region, state, county or city, which congressional committee or executive agency oversees a particular area of interest, the following works can be of assistance. Copies may be available in a local library or at a government depository library in your state.

Catalog of Federal Domestic Assistance. Washington, U.S. Government Printing Office, 1965– . 2 vols. looseleaf. Annual and update.

This provides extensive information about federal social and economic grant programs, including eligibility requirements and application procedures. An appendix gives addresses of state and regional offices of federal agencies and departments, many of which are authorized to distribute funds directly to the geographic areas in which they are located.

Consolidated Federal Funds Report. vol. I, county areas; vol. II, subcounty areas. Washington, U.S. Government Printing Office, 1984– . Annual.

Federal Expenditures by State. Washington, U.S. Government Printing Office, 1983– . Annual.

These companion volumes issued by the Bureau of the Census report on expenditures, obligations, grants and payments to state and local governments as well as grants to nongovernmental recipients. They are issued in March for the previous fiscal year.

United States Government Manual. Washington, U.S. Government Printing Office, 1935– . Annual.

This contains descriptions of the departments and agencies of the federal government, giving enabling legislation and functions of each, organization charts, names of major officers, and addresses of some state and regional offices.

Washington Information Directory. Washington, Congressional Quarterly, 1975/76– . Annual.

It describes departments and agencies of the executive branch of the federal government, congressional committees and groups, and national organizations with offices in Washington, D.C. Subject arrangement conveniently groups together government and private organizations with similar areas of interest. Current addresses and telephone numbers are given.

The primary source of government information produced electronically is the National Technical Information Service. Files are indexed in *Government Reports Announcements & Index* (NTIS, 1946– . Biweekly), which is available on CD-ROM and on-line through DIALOG and the Knowledge Index. This index also lists some publications of the Department of Energy's National Energy Information Center and the National Aeronautics and Space Administration Information Center. Complete listings of these publications are available in *Energy Research Abstracts* and *Scientific, Technical & Aerospace Reports*.

The National Archives contains historical materials including letters, census information, and war records. A librarian can help you determine whether this source is appropriate for your topic.

APPENDIX B
EXAMPLES OF
BIBLIOGRAPHY
ENTRIES AND
FOOTNOTES

This appendix lists examples of bibliography entries and corresponding footnotes for several common types of reference sources. Note the differences in word order. Bibliography entries list the author's last name first. Note also the differences in punctuation between footnotes and bibliography entries. Remember that your teacher may require certain bibliography and footnote styles that differ from those given here.

For reference sources not listed here, remember that the minimum information usually needed for a bibliography entry or a footnote is the author, title, place of publication, publisher, and copyright date. Your teacher or librarian can direct you to resources that tell how to cite less common reference sources.

BOOKS

ONE AUTHOR

Epstein, Edward Jay. *Counterplot*. New York: Viking Press, 1969.

[1] Edward Jay Epstein, *Counterplot* (New York: Viking Press, 1969), 37.

TWO AUTHORS

Blakey, G. Robert, and Richard N. Billings. *The Plot to Kill the President*. New York: Time Books, 1981.

[2] G. Robert Blakey and Richard N. Billings, *The Plot to Kill the President* (New York: Time Books, 1981), 50–53.

THREE AUTHORS

Kern, Montague, Patricia W. Levering, and Ralph B. Levering. *The Kennedy Crises: The Press, the Presidency, and Foreign Policy*. Chapel Hill: The University of North Carolina Press, 1983.

[3] Montague Kern, Patricia W. Levering, and Ralph B. Levering, *The Kennedy Crises: The Press, the Presidency, and Foreign Policy* (Chapel Hill: The University of North Carolina Press, 1983), 6.

ONE EDITOR

MacNeil, Robert, ed. *The Way We Were: 1963, The Year Kennedy Was Shot*. New York: Carroll & Graf, 1988.

[4] Robert MacNeil, ed., *The Way We Were: 1963, The Year Kennedy Was Shot* (New York: Carroll & Graf, 1988), 182–184.

EDITORS

Scott, Peter Dale, Paul L. Hoch, and Russell Stetler, eds. *The Assassinations: Dallas and Beyond: A Guide to Cover-ups and Investigations.* New York: Random House, 1976.

[5] Peter Dale Scott, Paul L. Hoch, and Russell Stetler, eds., *The Assassinations: Dallas and Beyond: A Guide to Cover-ups and Investigations* (New York: Random House, 1976), 350–353.

ONE COMPILER

Rice, William R., comp. *John F. Kennedy–Robert F. Kennedy: Assassination Bibliography.* Orangevale, Calif.: Rice, 1975.

[6] William R. Rice, comp., *John F. Kennedy–Robert F. Kennedy: Assassination Bibliography* (Orangevale, Calif.: Rice, 1975), 35.

COMPILERS

Guth, DeLloyd J., and David R. Wrone, comps. *The Assassination of John F. Kennedy: A Comprehensive Historical and Legal Bibliography, 1963–1979.* Westport, Conn.: Greenwood Press, 1980.

[7] DeLloyd J. Guth and David R. Wrone, comps., *The Assassination of John F. Kennedy: A Comprehensive Historical and Legal Bibliography, 1963–1979* (Westport, Conn.: Greenwood Press, 1980), 223–226.

TRANSLATED WORK

Gaulkin, Charles, trans. *The Oswald Affair: An Examination of the Contradictions and Omissions of the Warren Report by Leo Sauvage.* Cleveland: World Publishing Co., 1966.

[8] Charles Gaulkin, trans., *The Oswald Affair: An Examination of the Contradictions and Omissions of the Warren Report by Leo Sauvage* (Cleveland: World Publishing Co., 1966), 96–97.

BOOK IN A SERIES

Short, James F., Jr., ed. *Modern Criminals.* Transaction Society Book Series, no. 8. New Brunswick, N.J.: Transaction Books, 1973.

[9] James F. Short, Jr., ed., *Modern Criminals,* Transaction Society Book Series, no. 8 (New Brunswick, N.J.: Transaction Books, 1973), 86–87.

ENCYCLOPEDIAS

SIGNED ARTICLE

Kaufman, Burton I. "Cold War," *World Book Encyclopedia.* 1991 ed.

[10] Burton I. Kaufman, "Cold War," *World Book Encyclopedia*, 1991 ed.

UNSIGNED ARTICLE

"Lee Harvey Oswald." *Encyclopedia Americana.* 1991 ed.

[11] "Lee Harvey Oswald." *Encyclopedia Americana*, 1991 ed.

SIGNED ARTICLE ON CD-ROM

Kaufman, Burton I. "Cold War." *World Book Encyclopedia.* 1991 ed. CD-ROM. Chicago: World Book, Inc. 1991.

[12] Burton I. Kaufman, "Cold War," *World Book Encyclopedia*, 1991 ed., CD-ROM (Chicago: World Book, Inc., 1991).

MAGAZINES, JOURNALS, AND NEWSPAPERS

ARTICLE IN MAGAZINE

Fonzi, Gaeton. "Who Killed JFK?" *Washingtonian*. Nov. 1980, 200–215, 218–237.

[13] Gaeton Fonzi, "Who Killed JFK?" *Washingtonian*, Nov. 1980, 200–215, 218–237.

ARTICLE IN MAGAZINE ARCHIVED IN ON-LINE DATABASE

Fonzi, Gaeton. "Who Killed JFK?" *Washingtonian*. Nov. 1980, 200–215, 218–237. On-line. Dialog. 3 Oct. 1996.

[14] Gaeton Fonzi, "Who Killed JFK?" *Washingtonian*, Nov. 1980, 200–215, 218–237, On-line. (Dialog, 3 Oct. 1996).

ARTICLE IN JOURNAL

Bickel, Alexander M. "The Failure of the Warren Report." *Commentary*, vol. 42 (Oct. 1966): 31–39.

[15] Alexander M. Bickel, "The Failure of the Warren Report," *Commentary*, vol. 42 (Oct. 1966): 31–39.

ARTICLE IN NEWSPAPER

Oglesby, Carl, and Jeff Goldberg. "Did the Mob Kill Kennedy?" *The Washington Post*, 25 Feb. 1979, Bl, 4.

[16] Carl Oglesby and Jeff Goldberg, "Did the Mob Kill Kennedy?" *The Washington Post*, 25 Feb. 1979, Bl, 4.

GOVERNMENT PUBLICATIONS

CONGRESS

U.S. Congress. House. Select Committee on Assassinations. *Investigation of the Assassination of President John F. Kennedy.* Hearings, 95th Cong., 2nd sess., March 1979. Washington: GPO, 1979.

[18] U.S. Congress. House. Select Committee on Assassinations. *Investigation of the Assassination of President John F. Kennedy.* Hearings, 95th Cong., 2nd sess., March 1979 (Washington: GPO, 1979), 5.

INTERVIEWS

TELEPHONE INTERVIEW

Doe, John. Telephone conversation with Mr. Jackson, 19 October 1994.

[19] John Doe, telephone conversation with Mr. Jackson, 19 October 1994.

INTERVIEW IN PERSON

Doe, John. Personal interview with Mr. Jackson, 30 October 1994.

[20] John Doe, personal interview with Mr. Jackson, 30 October 1994.

FILMS

Schechter, Danny (director). *Beyond JFK: the Question of Conspiracy.* Burbank: Warner Home Video, 1992.

[21] Danny Schechter (director). *Beyond JFK: the Question of Conspiracy* (Burbank: Warner Home Video, 1992).

APPENDIX C
SAMPLE
REPORT

The sample report on the following pages contains a title page, a complete table of contents, an introduction, a conclusion, and a bibliography. It also contains one chapter from the body of the report.

WHO IS RESPONSIBLE FOR THE DEATH
OF JOHN FITZGERALD KENNEDY?

by

Chris Doe

American History 101
April 10, 1994

TABLE OF CONTENTS

INTRODUCTION

John F. Kennedy, thirty-fifth president of the United States, was shot to death in Dallas, Texas on November 22, 1963. To this day the motives, methods, and men linked with Kennedy's death remain a subject of controversy and a topic of debate. The controversy and debate persist because evidence cited in support of various theories is not only plausible but also logical. In this report the evidence offered to substantiate the three most widely accepted theories: the Lone Assassin Theory, the Organized Crime Theory, and the Cuban Theory, will be reviewed in order to determine which of these theories is the most logical and conclusive.

1

THE ORGANIZED CRIME THEORY

Leaders of local and national organized crime groups in the United States, often referred to as the Mafia, the Mob, or the Syndicate, and leaders of labor unions had individual as well as collective motives for plotting the death of John F. Kennedy. Among those individuals reputed to have had strong motives were Jimmy Hoffa, Carlos Marcello, and Sam Giancana. In order to understand the motives of these men, it is first necessary to note the tangled interrelations of these men and those others who are thought to have played a role in the assassination as well as to review certain events that preceded the assassination.

Before ascending to the presidency in 1961, John Kennedy and his brother Robert Kennedy served on the McClellan Committee, which was formed in 1957 to investigate labor racketeering and organized crime. Jimmy Hoffa, head of the Teamsters Union, and Carlos Marcello, head of the Mafia in the south-central region of the United States, were the main targets of the committee.

6

Both Hoffa and Marcello felt intense pressure as a result of the investigations into their business transactions and feared prosecution resulting in deportation or imprisonment. Either of these sentences would have stripped them of their considerable power and denied them access to their sizable fortunes. In 1961, Marcello's fears were realized when Robert Kennedy, attorney general of the United States, used the power of his office to arrange to have Marcello deported to Guatemala. As a result Marcello "... spoke of meting out Mafia justice to the Kennedys."[1]

When a second deportation order was upheld by the courts, after Marcello had illegally reentered the United States, the hatred that Marcello, his family, and associates felt toward Robert Kennedy escalated. Marcello stated that, "... if Bobby Kennedy were killed, the President would crack down on his brother's enemies--people like

---

[1]Anthony Summers, <u>Conspiracy</u> (New York: McGraw-Hill, 1980), 337.

himself and Hoffa... but if the President were killed, Lyndon Johnson would do nothing. And Bobby Kennedy, whom Johnson hated, would lose all his power."[2] Marcello further reasoned that "... President Kennedy had to go, but that he would have to arrange his murder in such a way that his own men would not be identified as the assassins ... he would have to use, or manipulate, someone not connected to his organization into a position where he would be immediately blamed by the police for the job. He had already thought of a way to set up a 'nut' to take all the heat, 'the way they do it in Sicily'."[3]

Marcello was not the only person to reflect upon how the death of John Kennedy would be of personal benefit. Jimmy Hoffa did so as well. "He was gravely concerned during the McClellan

---

[2]John H. Davis, _Mafia Kingfish: Carlos Marcello and the Assassination of John F. Kennedy_ (New York: McGraw-Hill, 1989), 93.

[3]Davis, 109-110.

Committee period over the effects of
the newspaper headlines on his wife and
children, who until then had been
shielded from his complex operations."[4]
Hoffa underlings "... worried for fear
that Kennedy [Bobby] might attempt to
shame his family, and for fear that the
boss would be unable to control his
volatile temper."[5] It was Hoffa who
reasoned that "... without John F.
Kennedy around, Robert F. Kennedy would
be 'just another lawyer'."[6]

Sam Giancana, boss of the Chicago
Mafia and a suspected accomplice in a
CIA-backed plot to kill Cuba's Fidel
Castro, also bore a grudge against the
President, his brother Robert, and
their father, Joseph Kennedy. The basis

---

[4]Walter Sheridan, The Fall and Rise of Jimmy Hoffa (New York: Saturday Review Press, 1972), 143.

[5]Ralph and Estelle James, Hoffa and the Teamsters (Princeton, N.J.: D. Van Nostrand Company, 1965), 21.

[6]Seth Kantor, Who Was Jack Ruby? (New York: Everest House, 1978), 28.

of Giancana's grudge can be traced back to a contribution he made to Kennedy's presidential campaign. Giancana mistakenly assumed his money would buy him and his cohorts amnesty from intense federal investigations. Giancana became angry and felt he had been betrayed when, after the election, the Kennedy brothers used their increased clout to intensify their relentless pursuit of organized crime figures. Members of the underworld in turn became equally as relentless in their efforts to curb the Kennedy brothers' pursuit of the Mob. Unable to restrain the Kennedys through money, the Mob decided to try to do so by taking advantage of John Kennedy's attraction to beautiful women.

Mob leaders planned to benefit from John Kennedy's weakness by gathering evidence to publicize his romantic trysts with the actress Marilyn Monroe, and with Judith Campbell Exner, aspiring actress and girlfriend of Sam Giancana. Kennedy's romantic liaisons with these beautiful women were secretly tape-recorded by members of the underworld with the intent of using the tapes to force Kennedy and his brother Robert, who had also been involved with Marilyn Monroe, to curtail their pursuit of organized crime.

It is widely known that Marilyn Monroe's "... association with Frank Sinatra brought her into the company of some of the Kennedys' most determined enemies. One of these was the Los Angeles organized crime boss, Mickey Cohen, who had links to Carlos Marcello ... and (who) had shared one of his girlfriends, the stripper Candy Barr, with Jack Ruby."[7]

Ultimately J. Edgar Hoover, then head of the FBI, pointed out to the president that his friendship with Sinatra and his romantic liaisons with Marilyn Monroe and Judith Campbell Exner put him in a compromising situation. Hoover's warning subsequently caused Kennedy to terminate his friendships with all three.

However, by that time Kennedy may have had the proverbial "three strikes

---

[7]Davis, 239.

against him." He had ostensibly angered the Mob 1) in his zeal to curb their power, 2) in his drive to confiscate their money, and 3) in his conquests of at least two of their women. As one observer noted at the time, "Kennedy violated the Mob's own code of ethics: 'It is well understood by prosecutors and police that there is a line that must not be crossed. You are all right as long as you do not sleep with them! You do not take favors, either money or sex. If you do, and then take action against them, retaliation awaits'."[8]

Whether Kennedy's assassination was an act of retaliation or a simple act of aggression to achieve a desired outcome is uncertain. What is certain is that Kennedy's death had a profound effect upon Robert Kennedy, whose consuming grief and lack of support from Lyndon Johnson adversely affected his drive and effectively diminished his power.

---

[8]Alan Adelson, The Ruby Oswald Affair (Seattle: Romar Books, 1988), 250.

Thus, the prophetic statements of Marcello and Hoffa concerning Robert Kennedy's loss of power and effectiveness in the event of the death of his brother, the president, became a reality.

Just as the events that preceded the assassination remain puzzling, so do those that immediately followed. In one of a bizarre series of events subsequent to President Kennedy's assassination, Jack Ruby shot and killed Lee Harvey Oswald. Ruby's act effectively ended all hope of obtaining a complete firsthand account of Oswald's actions and motives. Ruby himself then became the subject of speculation and investigation regarding his motives.

When the assassination investigation focused on Ruby, owner and manager of a Dallas, Texas, nightclub frequented by mobsters, it was discovered that his ties to organized crime dated back to his youth in Chicago. It was further discovered that in the two months before Kennedy's assassination Ruby engaged in numerous telephone conversations with organized crime figures including associates of Hoffa and Marcello. Consequently, to many, "the murder of Oswald by Jack Ruby had all the earmarks of an organized-crime hit, an action to silence the assassin, so he could not reveal the conspiracy."[9]

Thus, one realizes after extensive research and careful reading that members of the underworld were involved in varying degrees in influencing the activities and proclivities of John Kennedy from the dazzling days preceding his presidential election to the dark days following his assassination. These same men had speculated about life without President Kennedy, had contrived to control him, and very possibly had arranged his death.

---

[9]G. Robert Blakey and Richard N. Billings, The Plot to Kill the President (New York: Time Books, 1981), 339.

CONCLUSION

John F. Kennedy's assassination has undoubtedly been the most carefully scrutinized and thoroughly investigated murder ever to have occurred. Yet, decades later, the one and perhaps only aspect upon which there is widespread agreement is that the assassination involved a conspiracy. To this day the numerous events, facts, and participants remain shrouded in a fog created by collusion, corruption, and cover-ups. It is almost certain that we will never know all the details and circumstances pertaining to the assassination of John Kennedy. As the years have passed, the memories of witnesses have blurred; suspects, witnesses, and investigators have died; and the desire of the government and the people to pursue the matter has waned. The motives, methods, and men continue to be elusive. However, based upon the evidence and findings made public and discussed in this report, it can be concluded that members of organized crime bear the mass, if not

25

the entire, responsibility for the death of John F. Kennedy.

They had the motives. President Kennedy and his brother, through unrelenting pressure and investigations, had threatened their freedom, their fortunes, and their futures.

They had the methods. Decades of in-fighting and gang rivalry allowed these nefarious men to perfect the methods by which they murdered those who in any way threatened their livelihood.

They had the men. In an organization in which men deem murder and mayhem acceptable methods of settling their differences, there can be little doubt that organized crime leaders were capable of conspiring to have President Kennedy assassinated.

BIBLIOGRAPHY

Adelson, Alan. _The Ruby Oswald Affair_. Seattle: Romar Books, 1988.

Blakey, G. Robert, and Richard N. Billings. _The Plot to Kill the President_. New York: Time Books, 1981.

Davis, John H. _Mafia Kingfish: Carlos Marcello and the Assassination of John F. Kennedy_. New York: McGraw-Hill, 1989.

"The Death of the President," _Information Finder_. CD-ROM. Chicago: World Book, Inc., 1991.

Fonzi, Gaeton. "Who Killed JFK?" _Washingtonian_. Nov. 1980, 200–215, 218–237. On-line. Dialog. 3 Oct. 1996.

James, Ralph and Estelle. _Hoffa and the Teamsters_. Princeton, N.J.: D. Van Nostrand Company, 1965.

Kantor, Seth. _Who Was Jack Ruby?_ New York: Everest House, 1978.

Sheridan, Walter. _The Fall and Rise of Jimmy Hoffa_. New York: Saturday Review Press, 1972.

Summers, Anthony. _Conspiracy_. New York: McGraw-Hill, 1980.

27

GLOSSARY

Abbreviation. A shortened form of a word.

Almanac. An annual book containing statistics, dates, information about the moon, and other information that is different every year.

Annotation. A brief note, description, or abstract added to an index entry to indicate its extent or value.

Appendix. Additional material about a subject placed at the end of a report or a book.

Archive. An organized set of papers or records maintained for future research.

Atlas. A book of maps.

Bibliography. An alphabetical list of all the reference sources from which information for a report or a book was obtained.

Books in Print. An annual book that lists the titles of books currently in print. This publication can be found in virtually every library.

Call number. The number assigned to a book in a library collection.

Card catalog. An alphabetized listing (by title, author, and/or topic) of the books in a library collection. Many libraries also have an on-line catalog. Often only materials that the library has acquired more recently are listed in the on-line catalog; the card catalog is still maintained for older materials.

CD-ROM (*Compact Disk-Read-Only Memory*). A compact disk containing information that cannot be added to or erased and is accessed on a computer with a CD-ROM drive. Some contain the full text of an encyclopedia set and are accompanied by sound as well as both still and motion pictures.

Computer file. Information, such as a document or graphic, created in a software program and saved on the computer's hard drive or on a floppy disk.

Copyright date. The year in which a book was published.

Cumulation. New material added to an existing reference such as a periodical index for which monthly updates are issued in paper covers. Subsequent hardcover editions of the index include all the material in the cumulations.

Database. A computer file containing information organized in a logical fashion. Examples include the full text of encyclopedias and back issues of newspapers and magazines. Some databases are available on CD-ROM; many databases are available through on-line services. Fees are charged for using many databases.

Draft. The preliminary version of writing before the final copy.

Download. To transfer files from a remote computer to one you are using, typically when retrieving information from an on-line database.

Edit. To change a piece of writing by addition, deletion, or revision.

Footnote. A note at the bottom of the page on which a quotation appears identifying the source of the information.

Index. An alphabetical listing at the end of a book detailing the contents and the pages on which each listing can be found.

Index volume. The last volume in a set of encyclopedias which lists the contents and page numbers of information in preceding volumes.

Interlibrary loan. A method used to borrow a book that is not available at a local library.

Internet. A worldwide network of computer networks at educational, government, and research facilities and many businesses. Users can communicate and get access to almost any kind of information, from census statistics and historic speeches to bibliographical indexes and highly specialized databases on all subjects. It can be accessed through some on-line services or directly through some libraries, usually those at colleges. It is not known for its ease of use; software packages called "front ends," which simplify the process of finding specific information, are becoming more available.

Microfilm catalog. A system for storing printed material on film in a reduced size.

On-line service. A consumer computer service that provides communication utilities (such as electronic mail, bulletin boards, and forums or interest groups), current information (such as news, weather, and stock prices), services (such as travel reservations or financial analysis), and, most important, access to a range of databases. These databases typically include references such as encyclopedias, libraries of magazines and journals, and archives of consumer reports. Some provide access to the Internet. The best known are America Online, CompuServe, Prodigy, GEnie, Delphi, and Dow Jones News/Retrieval.

Outline. An organization of information by topics and subtopics.

Periodical. A magazine, journal, or other publication printed regularly, but not daily.

Plagiarism. The use of someone else's words, exactly as stated or written by that person, as your own.

Post. To send a message, usually by electronic mail, to an interest group on an on-line service.

Proofread. To read thoroughly to find and correct mistakes in content, spelling, grammar, and punctuation.

Quotation. The inclusion in your writing of someone else's words exactly as stated or written by that person. All quotations should have a footnote identifying the source.

Research report. An in-depth account about a specific topic.

Revise. To make changes in a written work to improve the quality and content.

Subtopic. The supporting details related to a main topic.

Table of Contents. A list at the beginning of a book detailing the organization of the chapters or topics of a book and giving the page numbers for each.

Thesaurus. An alphabetical list of words for which synonyms and antonyms are given.

INDEX